Crisis
COMMUNICATION

Expression of thanks

The authors would like to thank the following people for their much appreciated help: Bob Bellafiore, George Bogdanich, Lori C Booker, Myra J Borshoff, Barbara Casey, Colette Cornelissens, Lars Dagerholt, Susan A Davis, Ray D Eisenbrenner, Thor Erling Lund, Pamela D Evans, Amanda Farek, Michael Fineman, Rick French, Acácio Gomes, Bobbie Goodwin, Christian Hannestad, Eric Hess, Peggy Hubble, Raphael Hyslop, Carol Javaudin, Gwinavere Johnston, David Ketchum, Howard C Landau, Effie Lazaridou, Anita Lissona, Tim Loesch, Greg Loh, Anne McGregor-Lowndes, Ginny Melvie, Vibeke Mestanas, Virginia Miller, Debbie Mitchell, Laurey Peat, Daniel C Pinger, Mila Popova, Mary Beth Popp, Cindy Raymond, Don Rountree, Brad Rye, Katie Seigenthaler, David Stiefel, Renzi Stone, Mike Swenson, Jésus Timoteo Álvarez, Loredana Ulivi, Kaija Vataja, Pat Walsh, Ralf Weber, Dick Wertheim, Martin Westergaard, John Williams and Necla Zarakol.

Crisis
COMMUNICATION

● ● ● – – – ● ● ●

practical PR strategies for reputation
management and company survival

Edited by PETER F ANTHONISSEN

KOGAN
PAGE

London and Philadelphia

First published in Great Britain and the United States in 2008 by Kogan Page Limited

120 Pentonville Road
London N1 9JN
United Kingdom
www.koganpage.com

525 South 4th Street, #241
Philadelphia PA 19147
USA

ISBN 978 0 7494 5400 5

British Library Cataloguing-in-Publication Data

A CIP record for this book is available from the British Library.

Library of Congress Cataloging-in-Publication Data

Crisis communication : practical public relations strategies for reputation management and company survival / [edited by] Peter Frans Anthonissen.
    p. cm.
  Includes bibliographical references.
  ISBN 978-0-7494-5400-5
  1. Crisis management. 2. Corporations--Public relations. I. Anthonissen, Peter Frans.
  HD49.C738 2008
659.2--dc22

                        2008017599

Typeset by Saxon Graphics Ltd, Derby
Printed and bound in Great Britain by MPG Books Ltd, Bodmin, Cornwall

Contents

List of contributors

Peter Frans Anthonissen (Belgium) is an expert in the field of reputation management and crisis communication. He successfully advised the mergers of KBC, one of Belgium's leading banks, and the University of Antwerp; ensured the introduction to the stock market of different leading companies, and has advised Renault, Coca-Cola, Procter & Gamble, the Belgian and the Flemish governments and many other leading companies, organizations and personalities. Peter studied law at the universities of Antwerp, Leuven and Cambridge (Magdalene College). He was a lawyer, a consultant to members of the Belgian government and a journalist at the leading Belgian newspaper *De Standaard* and the financial daily *De Tijd* before he founded the communication consultancy Anthonissen & Associates in 1987. He has published several bestsellers and is visiting professor at universities in Belgium and abroad.

Roger Bridgeman (United States) has been in the public relations and communication business for more than 30 years. His field of experience extends from financial and professional services to high-tech, industrial and consumer marketing. He has represented Fortune 100 companies from Texas Instruments, Motorola, Microsoft, Kodak, Raytheon and Cisco, to new venture and overseas companies. During his career he has managed corporate crises and stakeholder issues – from corporate merges and acquisitions and competitor disinformation attacks, to technology-related consumer privacy issues. Prior to establishing

Bridgeman Communications in 1986, Roger worked for a number of leading public relations firms and international corporations including Ruder & Finn and General Electric. Roger holds a Bachelor of Science degree in public relations from Boston University's College of Communication, where today he is on the part-time faculty teaching Corporate Public Affairs in the graduate programme.

Marianne de Bruijn (The Netherlands) is an experienced PR consultant working for ACA/JES Communicatie (Amsterdam). Marianne studied communication management at The Hague School of European Studies and handles all kinds of PR and communication projects, including crisis communication. She acted as the spokesperson for the insurance company Ohra during the introduction of the new health insurance system in The Netherlands. She fulfilled the same role for the credit card company ING Card when credit card fraud cases or other issues occurred. For ACA/JES she advised telecommunications firm KPN Mobile in the campaign on UMTS. The campaign included informing the public, local authorities and real estate owners about the technical benefits of UMTS and reducing the public resistance towards UMTS. She also led the crisis communication project concerning the closing of a Dutch plant by a French company. This project was run in close cooperation with the management of the company in The Netherlands and France.

Willem Buitelaar (The Netherlands) has extensive experience in public relations and media relations. Before joining ACA/JES Communicatie (Amsterdam) as a senior consultant PR/PA, he worked in several public relations positions, in both the public and private sectors. He has been Head of Public Relations and spokesman for The Netherlands Board of Tourism (NBT), for which he coordinated crisis communication programmes when the reputation of The Netherlands as a tourist destination was at stake. Willem holds a degree in French Language and Literature and Mass Communications from the universities of Leiden and Utrecht (The Netherlands) and counsels private national and international companies and governmental bodies on general communication issues and recruitment PR.

Tom Gable (United States) is founder and CEO of Gable PR, a full service firm based in San Diego and with clients throughout the west. Prior to starting his firm in 1976, he was business editor of the *San Diego Tribune* and wrote for *The Wall Street Journal* and other business publications. He was a Pulitzer Prize nominee and holds many awards for writing and public relations. Tom has represented a range of clients from start-ups to Fortune 100 companies. He writes regularly for national business and marketing media on trends in public relations. He is working on the fifth edition of his *PR Client Service Manual*, sold through the Public Relations Society of America (PRSA), currently number one in its category. Tom speaks frequently at national conferences on trends in public relations, crisis communication, strategic planning and reputation management. He has received four Silver Anvils, the highest honour from PRSA. He was president of IPREX for two years and also chairman of the Counsellors Academy of PRSA.

Jerry Hendin (United States) was the first Vice-President of Communications for Boeing's Commercial Airplane Company and co-authored the first manual for the airline industry on crisis communication. Since then, Jerry has trained more than 30 airlines around the world on how to protect their businesses and their reputations in a crisis. After nearly 10 years at Boeing, where he was also the Vice-President, Public Affairs–International, Jerry became the president and CEO of Edelman Public Relations, Asia Pacific and continued working with regional companies on crisis management issues. He is currently the managing partner of Alliance Public Relations in Seattle, Washington, a small consultancy that helps companies worldwide build and protect their reputations around the world.

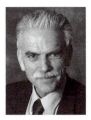

Stuart Hyslop (United Kingdom) held senior executive positions on *The Daily Mail* and *The Times* before starting Surrey House Corporate Communication Limited in 1985. He also worked on the London *Evening News*, the London *Evening Standard* and *The Sunday Times* in what was then referred to as Fleet Street. Stuart is a member of the Chartered Institute of Public Relations (CIPR), and Communicators in Business (CiB), and takes a sharp interest in their affairs. He writes, lectures, teaches and trains on a wide range of communication issues. He has trained, organized exercises and assisted senior executives in crises in the UK,

Europe and the Far East. His experience includes a wide range of utilities, transport, support services, insurance, risk management, government, food, retail and charities.

Nick Leighton (United Arab Emirates) is the founder and CEO of NettResults Public Relations, a leading independent media relations agency with offices across the Middle East and in California, United States. Since NettResults's conception in 1999, Nick and the NettResults teams have been assisting clients with crisis communication, both big and small. Nick is also the founder and CEO of NettResults Management Consulting, a California-based management company that specializes in exploration and mapping of companies to produce process maps. Nick studied Psychology of Human Communication at De Montfort University, Leicester, UK and then went on to gain an MBA with a speciality in marketing from Leicester Business School. He has worked in Eastern and Western Europe and the Middle East. He now divides his time between California and Dubai.

Robert J Oltmanns (United States) is the president of Skutski & Oltmanns, Inc, an independent public relations firm in Pittsburgh, Pennsylvania. Bob's unique background in environmental communication includes a combination of technical training and 25 years of professional public relations experience. He has been a counsellor on a variety of environmental public relations issues for clients in the chemical, nuclear, forest products, electric power and transport industries, among others. Bob is also an adjunct professor of environmental public relations at Duquesne University's Center for Environmental Research and Education. He holds degrees from Montclair State College in New Jersey and the University of Pittsburgh's Graduate School of Engineering, and is an accredited member of the Public Relations Society of America's College of Fellows and the PRSA Counsellor's Academy.

Steven Pellegrino (United States) returned to Kortenhaus Communications as an agency partner in September 2001 with 15 years experience in hospitality, restaurant and travel marketing. In his present role, Steven oversees the daily operations of the agency, supervises account teams, and develops strategic programming for existing clients while also generating new business. Steven serves as creative director for the agency and has successfully conceptualized and executed many high profile events including The Citi Performing Arts Center's 25th Silver Anniversary, Mayor Thomas M Menino's 2006 Inaugural Celebration, the Boston Red Sox 2004 Hall of Fame Dinner and the launch of The Container Store in both Chestnut Hill and Natick. Steven serves on various local boards including Boston Partners in Education and the Multicultural AIDS Coalition. He is active with Community Servings, an organization that delivers hot meals to individuals and families living at home with AIDS, is a member of the Human Rights Campaign Federal Club and is active with Children's Hospital League, Save Venice and the MSPCA (Massachusetts Society for the Prevention of Cruelty to Animals). He is a graduate of Boston College and resides in Boston's South End and Ogunquit, Maine.

Silvia Pendás de Cassina (Mexico) has been a communicator for the past 35 years in Mexico and has widespread experience in crisis and issues management. Silvia managed the Alaska Airlines Flight 261 case and worked closely with Boeing Commercial Airplanes and Alaska Airlines to support crisis management efforts in Mexico. She also supported crisis management issues after the terrorist attacks of 9/11 for her client Continental Airlines. She is currently President of Silvia Pendás, SA, a PR and communication firm based in Mexico, which is celebrating its 30th anniversary. Prior to joining Silvia Pendás, SA, she was Vice-President of two leading PR firms in Mexico. Educated in the United States and Europe, Silvia holds a Master's Degree in Italian and Linguistics from Georgetown University in Washington, DC. She is a member of Damas Publicistas de Mexico and the Public Relations Society of America, and is an honorary board member of Casa de la Amistad para Niños con Cancer, a non-profit organization dedicated to helping children with cancer in Mexico.

Nuria Sánchez (Spain), Executive Director of Quantumleap since 1997, is responsible for client relations, design and execution of communication strategies and PR plans. Previously, Nuria was Advertising and PR Manager of Editemo, an automotive editorial group and consultant in several market research companies. Nuria has lectured in different communication forums and seminars. She has a degree in Advertising and Public Relations and a Master's in Business Communication from Complutense, University of Madrid.

Elizabeth Seigenthaler Courtney (United States) is Chairman/CEO of Seigenthaler Public Relations, Inc in Nashville, TN. She serves as a consultant in the management of strategic communication programmes on behalf of the firm's clients. A graduate of Boston College with a degree in English and Communications, Beth joined SPR in 1987 after working with firms in Boston, MA and London, England. Elected President of the firm in 1997 and then CEO in 2004, Beth is recognized as a business and civic leader and holds such merits as Leadership Foundation Fellow by the International Women's Forum, top '40 Nashvillians under 40' by *Business Nashville* magazine, and Outstanding Volunteer of the Year by the Nashville Chamber of Commerce – where she served as an elected member of the executive board.

Thom M Serafin (United States) has established himself as one of the pre-eminent communication professionals in Illinois over the last 25 years, providing a host of successes for both public affairs and corporate clients. He often is called upon in crisis communication issues to direct and integrate diverse points of view into a strategic real-time programme for clients. It is that immediate real-time skill that distinguishes Thom from the competition. In the 1970s, Thom was the political/government correspondent for a state-wide radio network (IRN) focusing on politics and government. Thom later immersed himself in politics by handling press for a 1978 US Senate campaign. After moving back to the news side for two years as assignment editor of a TV and radio organization, Thom was asked to join the Washington press staff of Senator Alan J Dixon, returning to Chicago to handle Senator Dixon's successful 1986 US Senate campaign. Thom left Senator Dixon's staff in 1986 to set up his own political and corporate communications consulting firm, Serafin & Associates.

Tony Shelton (United States) is President of Shelton & Caudle, the crisis counsel and training division of Houston-based Vollmer Public Relations. In 16 years of consulting practice, he has counselled national and international clients on crises ranging from major explosions at industrial plants to investigations by news teams for the US television networks. As an example, Tony directed the development of an award-winning crisis communication programme for the US affiliate of a major French industrial company. The company deemed the programme a best practice and has implemented it in its facilities around the globe. He holds a Master's degree in journalism from the University of Missouri. Tony has been quoted frequently on communication topics in publications across the United States.

Kathryn Tunheim (United States) has extensive experience in corporate, government and non-profit communication management. In 1990 Kathy left her position as Vice-President of Corporate Communications and Internal Communications at Honeywell to found Tunheim Santrizos Company. Prior to her 10-year tenure at Honeywell, she was marketing communications manager for computer manufacturer NCR. Earlier she served as assistant press secretary to Wendell Anderson during his terms as Governor of Minnesota and his term as US Senator from Minnesota. As President and CEO, Kathy Tunheim oversees strategic planning for clients and is actively involved in client service and counselling. Under her leadership Tunheim Partners has grown to be one of Minnesota's largest public relations agencies.

Odile Vernier (France) is the Chairwoman and Executive Manager of Beau Fixe. After a career in journalism in Japan, Odile joined the staff of a French ministry. She then worked in a public relations agency before creating Beau Fixe in 1988, which she is now running as its President. Her fields of expertise range from sensitive communication to crisis communication: how to deal with rumours, social problems, environmental problems, product problems and company governance.

Tim Wallace (United States) has written, spoken and lectured about crisis communication both in the United States and in Europe in the course of a 25-year career. His client engagements include Ernst & Young, JP Morgan Chase, Citicorp, Deutsche Bank, Booz Allen Hamilton, Merrill Lynch, Katzenbach Partners, Beech-Nut, Kmart and Raymond James, among others. His unparalleled success in op-ed writing has led to numerous *Wall Street Journal* 'Manager's Journal' columns and *New York Times* op-eds under client by-lines. Mr Wallace has received numerous industry awards for programming excellence, including the Silver Anvil. He is a graduate of Emory University and holds a Master's degree from the University of Virginia.

Jim Walsh (Ireland) is Managing Director of Walsh Public Relations in Dublin, and has over 30 years experience in the Irish public relations and communication industry. He has been involved in all aspects of public relations, public affairs and media training with a wide variety of commercial organizations, government departments and representative groups. A Fellow of the Public Relations Institute of Ireland (PRII), he currently is President of IPREX, an international network of 58 independent public relations companies. A former President of the PRII and former Chairman of the Public Relations Consultants Association, Jim is the current treasurer of the Guild of Agricultural Journalists. He also writes and lectures on public relations issues.

Mania Xenou (Greece) has been the Managing Director of Reliant Communications since 2002. From 2000 to 2002 she was Regional Communications and Public Affairs Manager for Greece and Cyprus at Coca-Cola Hellas. From 1993 to 2000, she was the Manager of Corporate Affairs in Greece at Kraft Foods Hellas, and from 1988 to 1993 she was the Corporate Affairs Manager for Greece at Jacobs Suchard/Pavlides. From 1984 to 1988 she was responsible for barter contracts at an Athens-based international office. She is currently an associate instructor at the University of Panteion, Athens, in the Department of Communications and Media, where she teaches a course on crisis management. Mania holds a degree in Italian Literature and a degree in Business Administration and Organizational Behaviour.

Foreword

According 'Murphy's Law' whatever can go wrong, will go wrong (or, whatever can go wrong will go wrong, and at the worst possible time, in the worst possible way). Every CEO and senior executive should keep a copy of Murphy's Law prominently displayed on their desk to remind them to be ready to face its consequences.

The effect of Murphy's Law is not simply an error or situation which has to be put right. It can lead to irreparable damage to the reputation of an organization. Such damage can have financial, business and motivational implications which take years to redress.

While every issue or crisis has to be handled in a different way there is one common factor. That is the need for communication. Communication with staff, their families, customers, regulatory authorities, elected representatives and many other stakeholders.

In this era of always-on media, news and information about situations in Beijing, Sydney or San Francisco are known in Brussels, Moscow and Dubai within minutes.

With contributions from 22 international experts in the field of crisis communication and reputation management this book is a showcase of expertise, and involves an academically well-founded discussion on crisis communication. All these authors are connected to IPREX, (www.iprex.com), an organization of independent public relations agencies who provides clients with global reach while working with local expertise. IPREX has 60 leading independent firms who partner in major markets around the globe, in particular in Asia Pacific, EMEA and North America. The partner firms employ more than 800 professionals working in 27 countries.

The combination of the expertise of the writers and an international input has resulted in an exhaustive, professional and in-depth report on different types of crisis situation and their consequences. Because of the numerous examples and cases that demonstrate the practical side of the theories explained, the book will be a fruitful guide for CEOs, chairmen, general managers, marketing and communication officers, PR practitioners, students and many other interested parties in preparing for and coping with a crisis situation.

Being convinced of the importance of crisis communication and being well prepared is the key. Preparation is all...

Finally, I would like to extend a word of thanks to Peter Frans Anthonissen who is the father and editor of this book. He invented the whole concept, brought together all the authors, and encouraged and stimulated them continuously.

Jim Walsh
Worldwide President IPREX

Introduction

Senior management and leaders within companies, organizations and governments embroiled in a crisis have learnt the hard way what happens when the unthinkable becomes reality. An accident results in death or injury; a failed takeover causes the share price to plummet; toxic food, medicines or drinks lead to mass hysteria. All attention focuses on the guilty parties.

Inevitably, these crises are made public and are often grossly exaggerated by the media. If an organization produces a defective product, has an accident, a strike or an environmental disaster, the media can be expected to make this headline news within a matter of hours.

Every day, organizations run the risk of being affected. The fact that we live in an age of transparency means that no company or organization is immune to the threat of a possible crisis. Companies have become glass houses in which nothing can remain hidden. Everything is expected to be visible.

A crisis does not necessarily have to turn into a disaster for the business or organization involved. This book discusses how to limit damage effectively by acting quickly and positively. Moreover, it explains how to turn a crisis into an opportunity by communicating efficiently.

How an organization communicates when hit by crisis can often make or break it. We can all think of examples of this at both national and international level. Ironically, it is the very transparency referred to earlier – which many senior managers find so difficult to practise – that enables a company to create an image of openness. This is what stakeholders appreciate and trust the most. Preparation, speed, transparency and efficiency are the concepts that form this book's theme.

Crisis Communication has been written by a team of authors from a number of different countries. The fact that these authors are all experts in the field of crisis communication and reputation management makes this book a truly valuable asset, not least because it contains a wealth of international expertise. Numerous areas in which a crisis can occur are discussed. Throughout the book, we discover how the four key concepts mentioned above (preparation, speed, transparency and efficiency) are essential, whether it be in the food industry, during a takeover, a court case, or some calamity.

First and foremost, this book aims to warn managers that their business is not immune to crisis. If you are unprepared, there is a good chance that a crisis will bring an end to your company. Being convinced of the importance of crisis management and taking appropriate measures is essential. Secondly, we hope this book will serve as a guide to students and anyone wishing to learn more about crisis communication and reputation management.

Throughout all of the chapters, *Crisis Communication* demonstrates just how vital appropriate crisis communication is for every company. Each chapter illustrates a different aspect of this field of communication management.

In the first chapter, we become acquainted with crisis itself. Based on multiple examples, we discover typical characteristics of a crisis. The days when companies were only answerable to their own shareholders are long gone. Stakeholders are not only becoming more numerous; they are also more inquisitive and demand to be fully informed.

A crisis plan has become an indispensable asset in our fast-changing society. Immunity does not exist, but tackling crises and turning them into an opportunity is an art. Effective, fast communication can even strengthen a company's reputation. Stakeholders and the public judge a company by the manner in which a crisis is tackled. When human interests are placed before those of a business, the company is often granted a second chance. Reacting efficiently and effectively is the key imperative.

The need for crisis control forms the basis of Chapter 2. Companies can only benefit by controlling a crisis, hence the importance of developing a proactive crisis communication plan. Protect the reputation of the organization by communicating the right message, at the right time, to the right people, is the essential theme of this chapter.

First, and most importantly, the company must communicate the crisis management plan internally in an efficient and effective manner. What message is to be communicated? Who should communicate the message? To whom should the message be communicated? When should a press release be disseminated? Creating a good crisis communication team is the first step. Chapters 9 and 10 go into this in more detail, but this chapter illustrates how media contact deserves special attention. A media contact team is certainly not an unnecessary luxury. If internal communication flows smoothly, answers to the four questions above can then be sought.

The first step involves determining the targets. Who are the various stakeholders? Thereafter, what sort of information is required by each stakeholder and how can this be anticipated in advance? Furthermore, each stakeholder requires a different message. As already illustrated in the first chapter, a company must demonstrate its empathy with the crisis. Subsequently, if it appears that the company has the situation under control, then a certain reassurance ensues automatically. It is implicitly understood that speed plays a prominent role in this process.

A company with a good reputation has an advantage in times of crisis. The third chapter shows how companies with an impeccable track record and that make a positive contribution to the community are given the benefit of the doubt under less favourable circumstances. Building a good reputation is not something that happens overnight: it happens in a number of stages. Primarily, careful consideration must be given to the company's desired image. What are its core values? Are ethical standards of paramount importance? Or is the ethos all about slashing costs, making as much money as possible and riding rough-shod over staff and suppliers? Get the core values right and it is relatively easy to devise and implement a strategy aligned to these. Consistency and creativity are required to maintain and strengthen these values such that the image becomes a part of the corporate strategy. From research and the author's own experience, we are offered eight cornerstones to serve as guiding principles.

Unpredictability is a foremost characteristic of crisis. The fourth chapter, dealing with calamities, makes this readily apparent. Natural disasters and air crashes are good examples of this. In the first section, we see that an airline's communications are often erratic. The communications team is usually located at the company's head offices. This causes problems whenever an accident happens in another country, and certainly whenever there are language barriers.

The lesson is that an airline or similar organization with far-flung operations should have a crisis communication plan for every level and every location. This chapter presents case studies on Alaska Airlines 261 and Superquinn, demonstrating how the way in which a company reacts to a crisis often has more influence on public perception than the crisis itself. Additionally, this chapter deals with how to take into account the risks presented by natural disasters and the weather.

In Chapter 5, the new dynamics of financial crises are analysed. Additionally, we come to the realization that all types of crises discussed in this book have something in common: they have a major impact on a company's financial situation and, in turn, lead to a financial crisis. This chapter studies the financial consequences of a crisis and shows how these can be best tackled.

Fraud occurs in various guises. An organization may, justly – or unjustly – be accused of fraud. Chapter 6 shows how such accusations strike at the very heart of a company. Once fraud is discovered it can lead rapidly to legal problems. It is essential to demonstrate that the charge is unfounded, or that the matter is being investigated in a transparent fashion.

The first step involves investigating the facts. In the event that the accusations are true, it is important to distinguish between intentional and unintentional fraudulent practice. Clear public statements are very important in this respect. Once again, studies of real cases show that the way in which such accusations are dealt with often has more impact than the accusation itself. When someone is falsely accused of fraud, the facts must first be ascertained and then communicated quickly to the public. Subsequently, short- and long-term strategies must be developed to demonstrate that this person was actually the victim, not the perpetrator.

In the seventh chapter, we deal with communication about company reorganization and restructuring. These events always contain the seeds of a potential crisis and shareholders, where they exist, and staff must take precedence. Good communication plays the lead role. In this chapter, the authors evaluate how the chances of a reorganization/restructuring failing or succeeding are influenced by the communication activity surrounding it. This can be further complicated when, as outlined here, it involves cross-border sites.

Food quality and safety controls have vastly improved in recent times. We are becoming ever more aware of what we eat and it is no wonder that a food crisis has a major impact. Chapter 8 studies several food crises that have affected us over the past few years and the impact these had on our eating habits. We also look at how obesity is becoming more prevalent worldwide and how the food industry is playing a major role in combating it.

The author states that all businesses in this sector are in dire need of a crisis plan – more so than in any other. A proactive crisis plan covering all scenarios is essential for every food company. Stakeholders demand reassurance where it concerns food. Clear and credible information from such companies is crucial. Once again, the media plays a vital role. The case study of the *Prestige* ship disaster demonstrates the way in which a food safety crisis can arise.

As this book clearly illustrates, the media wield huge influence in any society. Almost daily, there are examples of how the media have the power either to play down or exacerbate a crisis. In Chapter 9, we learn how to deal with negative media. Preparation is half the battle. In addition, there are tips to help formulate a well-founded response or comment. Working proactively is the obvious route: continuously seek out potentially negative reports so you can prepare your response and take damage limitation measures. The international impact of the media is illustrated in the case study of damage control in the Low Countries.

Training is essential if you ever need to speak to the media or go on television or radio. It is crucial that you are prepared for this if a crisis erupts. In such an event it is best to work with a spokesperson who knows the ropes. In Chapter 10, we become better acquainted with the media and examine the recommended approach when dealing with journalists or broadcasters.

In the next chapter we address the role of the board of directors. Board members are often difficult to train: they are too busy, do not see the point of crisis training, or they do not dare expose themselves. The author of Chapter 11 provides real examples to demonstrate that the role of senior management in a crisis is crucial and how, if they are not properly trained and prepared, they can make things infinitely worse.

If a business problem develops into a legal dispute, this can have a devastating impact on a company. The case study presented in Chapter 12 shows that the interests of the various parties involved must be analysed, that the reputation management team must be conversant with the legal system and the media, and that all communication should use clear and concise language.

Sustainable enterprise is a priority for businesses. Companies that operate in an environmentally responsible manner improve their reputation. As a result of past environmental disasters caused by industry, we are now better prepared for such crises. Yet preparation and speed remain indispensable. Chapter 13 offers tips that all companies should observe.

Chapter 14 focuses on the internet, a source of constant and instantaneous information. The internet creates many new opportunities and challenges, but it also presents risks for those responsible for communication. Stakeholders are more readily inclined to take the initiative, and place and search for information online. Chapter 15 summarizes some of the pitfalls with which public relations professionals are confronted and how they deal with these.

The role of risk manager is relatively new in most large companies, but it is a position that is gradually carrying more weight. In Chapter

16, the role and the benefits of having a risk manager in a rapidly changing business environment are detailed.

Finally, in Chapter 17, crisis communication checklists are provided. These will help you, should you ever have the misfortune to be confronted with a crisis.

If my co-authors and I have succeeded in convincing you and your organization of the absolute necessity for proactive crisis communication and proper planning, then the objectives of this book will have been met. 'Forewarned is forearmed!'

Peter Frans Anthonissen

1 No thrillers, but hard reality

Crisis in all its forms

Peter Frans Anthonissen (Belgium)

Introduction

Crises have always been with us. They take companies and organizations by surprise, and they take on a host of forms. If we relive and review a series of noteworthy crises, we are able to draw up a list of general rules to act by. That arsenal of principles must be followed absolutely if – once you've been confronted with a crisis – you want to stand a real chance of surviving.

Unfortunately, we have an embarrassment of riches when it comes to examples of crises. The world has been hit by a remarkable number of crisis situations over the past few years. The tsunami that issued an unmistakable wake-up call to the world on 26 December 2004, for example. That enormous tidal wave, originating close to the island of Sumatra, claimed approximately 225,000 victims. The northern point of Sumatra was particularly hard hit, with 60 per cent of the city of Banda Aceh being destroyed by the tsunami, killing more than 200,000 people in that city alone.

Hurricane Wilma in October 2005 destroyed large sections of Mexico and Cuba, killed 62 people and caused more than €20 million in damage. In August of the same year, Hurricane Katrina, which ravaged the city of New Orleans and large portions of the state of Louisiana, killed more than 1,600 people. Hurricane Rita, one month later, raged over Louisiana, leaving approximately 120 people dead. The Norwegian oil tanker *Tricolour*, which collided with a container ship near the coast of France in December 2002, dumped approximately 178,000 litres of heavy oil into the ocean.

The list of product recalls is getting longer all the time. Coca-Cola, Jupiler, Amstel and Olvarit are only a few of the food companies that have had to take their products off the shelves. Auto manufacturers, such as Ford and Mercedes, and toy manufacturers that brought poisonous dolls to market, saw themselves forced to recall their products from the market temporarily.

Restructurings are a daily fact of life. If a factory closure, a merger, a split-up or relocation are not professionally prepared or executed, major difficulties can arise. The closure of Renault Vilvoorde and the termination of all activities of Marks & Spencer on the European mainland are prime examples. Strikes and other social actions are on the daily menu. Other forms of crises can also hit a company's human resources department, such as bullying that leads to the suicide of a member of staff.

It almost goes without saying that publicly listed companies are extra-sensitive to bad news. The dotcom madness that dominated all the stock markets in the recent past was responsible, in the first place, for the largest increase in dollar millionaires ever recorded. The fall of those internet and other IT companies was equally fast, if not faster. Internationally, major brands such as Yahoo, Amazon and a large number of other new gods, suffered heavy losses.

Politics also has its share of crisis situations. Crises are an essential component of the political world. Party politics is, in fact, a political conflict model. The House of Commons in Britain is the best illustration of the point: the members of parliament of the majority and the minority parties sit facing one another. It is therefore reasonable to conclude that crisis situations in political life are desirable, planned or created. This is an essential difference with business. Competing companies also torment one another mercilessly, but management is primarily concerned with avoiding crisis situations or, if possible, preventing them entirely. It is in a company's interest to function well.

Well-known figures are more likely to be the target of a crisis than mere mortals. Bill Gates, for example, the chief of Microsoft and one of the richest men in the world was the victim of a pie-thrower in Brussels. In and of itself, a rather insignificant event, but the video imagery and the photographs were broadcast and printed around the world.

Crises strike everywhere, including sport. On 29 May 1985 the European football championship final between Juventus and Liverpool was to have been a football party, but turned into a drama. A combination of blind fanaticism, panic and failing security measures resulted in 38 fatalities and nearly 400 wounded spectators in the Heysel Stadium in Brussels.

There are no guarantees

These and other disasters and accidents have made both companies and governments realize that they must be prepared for a crisis at all times. No one is assured that he or she will be spared. A permanent state of crisis awareness is therefore a fundamental requirement for every company or organization; but that is not enough. In the event of a crisis, effective and efficient communication can be a matter of life and death: what has really happened and what measures have been taken to deal with the crisis? If a company fails to follow the fundamental principles of crisis communication, the consequences can be far-reaching and disastrous.

The dioxin crisis that struck in Belgium in April 1999 led directly to the defeat of the Christian Democratic Party in the elections of 13 June 1999. Its defeat meant that it was not part of the governing coalition for the first time since 1958. Companies, too, that do not follow the essential principles, can find themselves in great difficulties. The shipping company Townsend Thoresen, for example, felt that it had to throw its name overboard after the sinking of the ferry the *Herald of Free Enterprise* in 1987 because the name seemed to be cursed forever.

For corporate leaders, it may be a hard fact to face, but the chance that they will be confronted with one major crisis or another has never been as great as it is today. Why? What elements cause crises? Human errors and mistakes, lapses in judgement, failure to react in time, failure to anticipate, mechanical faults or simply the refusal to face the fact that crises can strike anyone. With all of that, you would have to be blind not to be aware that company management will sooner or later be faced with a serious crisis. And let's be honest: a crisis does not have to be large in scope to be dangerous.

Why do crises strike more frequently today than in the past? We live in a highly developed society with access to a vast arsenal of high-tech resources. Computers lead and guide us on land, at sea and in the air. Some say that we all learn from our mistakes; experience has shown, however, that nothing could be further from the truth. The omnipresent technology means that the chance of a crisis situation arising is greater than it has ever been. The pharmaceutical company B-Braun can speak from experience. The medicines it produces are automatically packaged in sterile containers; there is no human intervention. A computer error led to four doses of potassium chloride being placed in ampoules that were intended for glucose. The ampoules were given to two newborn babies on 13 and 15 January 1999 in the Gasthuisberg University Hospital in Louvaine. They died within hours.

Are more accidents taking place than, say, 20 or 30 years ago? Most definitely not. But the environment has fundamentally changed. The role of the media has increased significantly. The chance that an incident escapes the attention of the all-seeing eyes of the journalists has become significantly smaller. But also, and especially, companies and managers are faced with new, major and additional responsibilities.

Stakeholders are everywhere

In a manner of speaking, corporate managers in the 1970s and 80s were only responsible to their shareholders and, in a couple of instances, their 'co-workers' as modern employers call their employees. Today, however, companies are being scrutinized constantly. Little of what companies do – or fail to do – escapes the attention of the many stakeholders. For, it is true, in addition to the shareholders, there is a whole slew of other parties who are involved with the company, or more aptly, feel involved with what companies do: trade unions, environmental associations, animal rights organizations, action groups of all kinds, the unavoidable TV, radio and printed press, the bloggers, but also, bankers, financial analysts, securities watchdogs, governments and parliaments with investigative commissions. In short, there is a virtually infinite constellation of directly and indirectly involved parties.

In addition, companies now live with a constantly expanding and increasingly complex battery of legislation. This is the case at more and more levels: in addition to the municipal and the provincial, there are regional and federation jurisdictions. Standing above all of those is the national or federal administration with, in turn, supranational policy bodies above them. The world is our village: companies are increasingly dominated by global players such as the World Bank, the International Monetary Fund, and the World Trade Organization.

The accountability factor

The whole range of international treaties and supranational legislation must be imposed, implemented and monitored nationally. Innumerable civil servants in ministries and departments fill their days with these activities. Inspection services check on the goings on at companies. Here, too, significant new trends arise that have an immediate impact on the crisis-sensitivity of a company. The creation of the

Euro zone, for example, the European Central Bank and the introduction of the Euro as the only currency in 13 European member states meant that there were new legislative and *de facto* rules of the game. Corporate leaders – willingly or otherwise – must deal with that situation.

The creation of Euronext as the first transnational stock exchange (grouping the markets of Brussels, Amsterdam, Paris and Lisbon) meant that increasing demands for transparency were placed on publicly traded companies. While it may be true that rules of good governance are promoted with heart and soul, living up to those rules leaves a lot to be desired in many companies.

The fact is that companies and other professional organizations will be increasingly confronted with the accountability factor. Certain aspects of the corporate responsibilities of corporate leaders, not only managers but also company auditors, accountants, lawyers and other advisers and consultants will clash. The new corporate responsibilities will be increasingly accounted for publicly. It almost goes without saying that when a company is faced with a crisis in that area, a broad range of public groups will demand immediate accountability over what has happened. And those public groups – who collectively form the often elusive but usually crucial public opinion – will want to know what will be done to deal with the crisis and solve the problems.

Annoying threats

Most crises develop with great alacrity, and news of the crisis travels around the world with the same speed. Companies that have not equipped themselves to deal with a crisis risk being confronted with a whole series of particularly annoying threats:

- boycotts of the company's products or services;
- collapse of the share price;
- serious legal claims;
- the loss of credit;
- possible bankruptcy;
- serious damage to the company's image and reputation;
- threatened loss of corporate senior and middle management;
- possible closure of the company or parts of it.

Following the negative publicity concerning the alleged dumping of the Brent Spar drilling platform in the North Sea in 1995, the Shell oil company was boycotted by German and Dutch activists. That led to loss of sales of 15 per cent and more.

Companies in crisis will find themselves facing one or more of these serious consequences. Companies that are well prepared and armed will survive even the most serious crisis. Not only that, they will emerge even stronger than before. Coca-Cola, Shell, Renault, Perrier and a host of others have proved that. How did they do it?

The history of crisis communication in business is still in its infancy, but there is already a case that is often referred to as an example of the proper and successful way of dealing with a crisis: the Tylenol affair. Tylenol is a fever and pain medicine that was developed by Johnson & Johnson, the large US pharmaceuticals group. For various reasons, Johnson & Johnson has assumed a prominent place in the history of crisis communication: it was the first time that a well-known company was confronted publicly with a major crisis. In addition, Johnson & Johnson dealt with the crisis so efficiently that its approach was praised by everyone after the fact and deserved all the credit it got. What exactly was the crisis that caused Johnson & Johnson to shake to its very foundations?

On 29 and 30 September 1982, several people died in the US city of Chicago after taking Tylenol tablets that had been filled with cyanide. At that time, Johnson & Johnson had more than one-third of the pain and fever medicine market, with its successful product, Tylenol. In practice, that meant turnover of US $450 million (€530 million), which represented 15 per cent of the company's profit. In the first phase of the crisis, the deaths were directly linked to the presence of cyanide in the tablets. As soon as the news was disseminated more widely there was a suspicion that no fewer than 250 deaths and cases of illness could be attributed to the poisoned Tylenol tablets. When the US media began to dig deeper into the matter and the public gained access to more and more information, the figure of 2,500 victims was being reported, both for deaths and illness.

Johnson & Johnson immediately began investigating 8 million Tylenol tablets. The tests showed that 75 tablets contained cyanide. All of those tablets originated – not coincidentally – from the same production batch. Ultimately, seven people died after ingesting the poisoned tablets, all of them in and around Chicago. Because news of the crisis had spread across the country like wildfire, 94 per cent of consumers made a direct connection between Tylenol and poisoning.

After the affair was over, Johnson & Johnson reintroduced the product. A mere five months after the terrible incidents, the pharmaceutical company had succeeded in regaining 70 per cent of its previous market share.

Crises are challenges

Johnson & Johnson used a well-considered approach in dealing with the crisis. The company positioned itself to the public as a defender of consumer interests and behaved as a good citizen by effectively assuming its responsibilities as a company. Furthermore, Johnson & Johnson communicated openly, directly and rapidly throughout the crisis.

How did Johnson & Johnson do that precisely? There is, after all, no guarantee that you will be able to turn a crisis into an opportunity. Johnson & Johnson acted on the basis of the worst conceivable scenario and applied all of the principles of successful crisis communication. To start with, the pharmaceutical company did not lose any valuable time: Tylenol was immediately recalled from all points of sale. All those who prescribed the drug – physicians, health insurers and pharmacists – were alerted and informed of the dangers of the product. By putting the consumer absolutely and unconditionally first, Johnson & Johnson took a great, but calculated risk. The company owed that to itself morally: its creed mandated that top priority always be given to the safety of the consumer. There is, of course, no guarantee that the corporate creed would be translated effectively into practice. The recall of all Tylenol tablets could, after all, have led to major losses. Johnson & Johnson remained true to its mission statement at all times, however.

The Tylenol affair is a perfect illustration of the expression that 'crises are challenges': regardless of how large the problem was, Johnson & Johnson discovered the opportunity that it contained. The company believed that the large-scale recall operation it had decided on could also be played out as an excellent marketing component after the fact. Johnson & Johnson quickly found a way to do this: when it reintroduced the product, it was the first in the pharmaceuticals industry to do so with safety packaging. Furthermore, the company was the first to put into practice the provisions of several pieces of legislation that had recently been introduced by the Food and Drug Administration, the US government standards body for medical products.

By removing Tylenol immediately from all sales points, Johnson & Johnson clearly communicated that the company was really concerned about public health. It would have been a painful mistake if the company had chosen the other option: to turn away, to stick its head in the sand, thinking, 'This, too, shall pass.' Exxon, for example, made precisely that mistake after the disaster with the *Exxon Valdez* in Alaska on 24 March 1989.

Johnson & Johnson could have taken yet a third path, by recalling Tylenol on a limited scale, primarily in Chicago and the surrounding area. That would have substantially limited the cost of the recall, which had, of course, serious financial implications – the cost of a massive recall, stocking and destroying a product cannot be overestimated. Johnson & Johnson rejected that third option in order to remain true to its corporate creed of making the safety of the consumer its top priority, whatever the cost.

It was very sensible of Johnson & Johnson to not go with a limited recall. If Tylenol had only been recalled in Chicago and the surrounding area, and remained on sale in the rest of the United States, many more alleged complaints would have been registered. Such a cascade of complaints often results in mass hysteria: patients are in a state of total uncertainty and lose their trust in the product's manufacturer. Such mass hysteria would have caused incalculable damage to Johnson & Johnson.

The Tylenol case provides us with several general principles for successful crisis communication. These are discussed below.

Successful crisis communication – principles

Always assume the worst-case scenario

If your company is confronted with a serious crisis, base your approach on the worst-case scenario, a scenario in which everything that can go wrong does go wrong. Do not assume that nothing will happen. Act on the basis of the disaster scenario.

What advantages does the development of a worst-case scenario offer? If you act on the basis of a scenario in which everything goes wrong, you will have taken all potential problems into account. The public will not be able to blame you, if panic arises, because the company is faced with unforeseen surprises. At most, they could say that you were too cautious or overstated the importance of the case. Furthermore, the chance that you generate respect and sympathy among the public if you take extensive measures is greater. On the other hand, a company that does not do enough to deal with a crisis will be branded as insensitive, uninterested, only focused on its own interests or cash flow, which is a situation that will cause irreparable damage to the company image and reputation and which should, therefore, be avoided at all costs.

Ensure that you have a plan

The crisis communication plan is an essential tool in dealing with a crisis, disaster or accident. Every company, regardless of the sector that it operates in, the type of activity or size of the company, should have an up-to-date crisis communication plan. When the Tylenol crisis broke, Johnson & Johnson already had a fully elaborated plan and the crisis was contained in a professional way. Drawing up a crisis communication plan requires the company management to think about potential disaster scenarios, regardless of how painful they can be. It is an ideal intellectual exercise.

At every phase of a crisis situation – from the moment that it breaks, during the rescue and communication responses, up to the evaluation – the company image, reputation and its good name and renown are at risk. The adage applies that it takes years of hard work to build up a good name, and a great deal of energy devoted to keeping it, yet it can be destroyed in an instant. If you respond too late or poorly to a crisis, it will cost you blood, sweat and tears to rebuild your good reputation. That's if it's not too late, that is, and your company has not gone under or had to divest major parts of its operations.

Don't lose any time

Johnson & Johnson's Tylenol crisis is a textbook example of a proper response and a successful resolution to a crisis situation. Union Carbide presents us with another example.

The chemical company Union Carbide (since the takeover on 6 February 2001, part of the giant Dow Chemical Company) was confronted with an extremely serious crisis and responded to it in a professional way. On 3 December 1984, shortly after midnight, a large quantity of poisonous gas escaped from an underground tank installation of the local Union Carbide factory in the Indian city of Bhopal. The gas formed a deadly cloud that spread over an area 20 square kilometres in size. Several hours later, as morning approached, gas was still escaping from the leaking tank. By that time, more than 1,200 people had already died. They suffocated in their sleep when they inhaled the extremely poisonous gas. Twenty thousand others were dealing with serious breathing and blood circulation problems. The gas, methyl isocyanate, is an important component in pesticides that are used in large quantities in Indian agriculture. The pesticides were manufactured in the Bhopal factory that was owned by the Indian subsidiary of Union Carbide.

As soon as news of the disaster reached the US headquarters of Union Carbide in Danbury, Connecticut, a worldwide halt to the production and transport of the gas was announced. Union Carbide immediately sent a medical specialist and a team of technicians to India to investigate the cause of the fatal leak. One day later, the chairman of Union Carbide, Warren Anderson, flew personally to Bhopal to see first hand what the situation was and to lead the investigation. That initiative was not without risk, however. At that moment, Union Carbide was already responsible for 1,200 deaths. The possibility that the man would be arrested on the spot when he arrived in Bhopal was not inconceivable. It was fitting that the management of Union Carbide took that risk.

By 7 December 1984, four days after the disaster had begun, the death toll had risen to more than 2,000. The number of seriously ill and badly injured casualties also kept rising. Bhopal had in the meantime been overrun by journalists, representatives of environmental associations, local politicians and experts – real or imagined – on poisonous gases. Bhopal was suddenly a well-known name around the world and the disaster was front-page news, and remained so for more than a month. The management of Union Carbide were bombarded with questions that it was almost impossible to provide answers to in the early days. That did not stop the journalists from continuing to ask questions about the causes of the accident and all aspects of the disaster, regardless of whether they were near by or far away. What was safety like at the factory? Is it acceptable to build a dangerous chemical factory in a densely populated residential neighbourhood? Who was responsible for the disaster? Will the victims and their families be able to file damage claims? Due to the lack of satisfactory answers to those questions politicians, journalists and so-called experts sent a tidal wave of guesses and speculation around the world. In retrospect, many of the articles and reports in the initial hours and days were based on vague eyewitness accounts and stories. The messages contained inaccuracies and outright errors, which caused significant damage to the corporate image of Union Carbide.

Even in the case of major dramas and disasters that occur at lightning speed, as was the case in Bhopal, it is not impossible to respond quickly. Union Carbide saw that perfectly. Several hours after the disaster, the company organized a press conference in the United States. The hotel in Connecticut was filled to the rafters with journalists. They fired off the standard questions, with a shocked undertone: How could this happen? Who is responsible? How many casualties are there? Will they be compensated? The speakers at the press conference themselves had little information available, hardly surprising given how recently everything had taken place. They were under a great deal of pressure, and they were not alone in that. The journalists also felt the hot breath of their editors on their neck to come up with a spectacular article or a solid report.

Union Carbide had prepared itself for that eventuality and was able to make several general statements. The management informed the journalists that they had immediately sent a medical specialist with medicine and respirators to Bhopal and that the physician had a great deal of experience in dealing with cases of methyl isocyanate inhalation. That news was later augmented with the official statement that a team of technical experts had also departed for India to investigate the factory and to ascertain precisely what had gone wrong. The management of Union Carbide took the victims of the disaster into consideration immediately and communicated that to the media in order to create the goodwill that was required.

People always come first

That brings us to the following important principle in dealing with a crisis. It is essential that companies clearly show their concern about the incident and the consequences for all the people involved. Union Carbide did that explicitly by sending the company's senior executive to the site of the disaster to gain first-hand information about the situation and to show his sympathy for the victims. By doing so, Union Carbide demonstrated what many other companies in crisis situations sometimes allow themselves to forget: human interests always take priority. In times of crisis, always ensure that a senior executive is available to show the company's concern and to explain what the company plans to do to reduce the suffering and to deal with the crisis.

Speed

Speed is also one of the keywords in dealing with a crisis. Companies should take control of the situation as quickly as possible. The company that has been hit by a disaster is seen as the only authoritative source of information. Only they can credibly inform public opinion – via the media – about the causes of the disaster and the steps that will be taken to deal with the crisis. Union Carbide did that by immediately organizing a press conference and announcing a string of measures that had been taken.

This cannot be emphasized enough: in times of crisis it is essential to communicate effectively and efficiently. Public opinion, after all, will pass judgement on the name and reputation of the company. In other words, companies are judged as harshly on the communication about the crisis as they will be about the crisis itself. It is therefore of the utmost importance to appreciate the vital role that communication plays in keeping a crisis under control.

Learn lessons from what has happened

Once the crisis has passed, the company can breathe more easily once again. That does not mean that it can consider the crisis to be fully over and filed away as a black page in its history. On the contrary: valuable lessons can be learnt from a crisis... lessons that must be shared with the company's own employees and with colleagues in the sector in order to prevent a similar crisis in the future. Every corporate leader with an ounce of common sense monitors disasters in his or her sector closely and learns lessons from them: 'That problem could also strike my company. How would we respond?'

The actions that personnel must take in the event of a crisis should, ideally, be looked at interactively in advance: role-playing and simulations to mirror reality sufficiently to identify potential difficulties in dealing with a crisis. Such activities show both the internal community and the outside world that the organization is aware of the possibility of a crisis. It is wrong to think that such things will create suspicion among personnel and other stakeholders; on the contrary, crisis awareness begets trust.

A crisis for every day of the week

The company guaranteed never to be confronted with a crisis does not exist. All companies are vulnerable, in all sectors. The potential for disasters and calamities is therefore virtually infinite.

The food sector

Companies in the food industry are extremely susceptible to problem situations. An error in the production process, incorrect quantities of a specific ingredient, the remains of cleaning products that have ended up in food... a small mistake can have major consequences. Product crises regularly result in the recall of the products affected.

In November 1993, Nutricia found remains of a much-used disinfectant in its jars of Olvarit baby food with beef and pork. The quantities found far exceeded the legally allowed quantities. It was not clear just how dangerous the substance was. Nutricia chose discretion as the better part of valour and recalled 2 million jars of Olvarit baby food from the shelves.

Ironically, the company, which monitored the hygiene and quality of its products extremely closely, had become a casualty of its own caution. Nutricia had cleaned the jars so thoroughly that traces of the disinfectant had remained behind in the jars. The damage is estimated to have cost more than €20 million.

Two months earlier, 350,000 jars of baby and child food of the Dutch brand Frisolac had been pulled from the shelves. Small particles of aluminium, which could have endangered the health of the children, had been found in the food.

In August 1993, glass splinters were found in several bottles of Heineken beer that were intended for export. It was a life-threatening situation, but fortunately there were no casualties. Heineken launched an investigation into the cause of the incident. It quickly became apparent that the company itself was not to blame. During packaging or opening, minute glass particles had come loose on the inside of the neck of the bottle. Heineken held the supplier of the bottles, United Glass Manufacturers, of Schiedam, responsible for the damage. In total, Heineken recalled 3.4 million bottles. At the end of March 1994, Jupiler beer was faced with a similar problem. There, too, the error lay with the bottle manufacturer, in this case Verlipac.

Unilever, a great name in the food industry, has not avoided crises. At the beginning of the 1950s, Unilever was the first to introduce plant-based margarine in the market, under the brand name Planta. Seven years after the product had been introduced, the company decided to add the anti-splash emulgator ME 18 to the margarine, with disastrous results. In the summer of 1960, more than 100,000 residents of The Netherlands suffered what became known as the blister disease, a type of skin rash. Four people died and hundreds of others were admitted to hospital. Unilever announced a total halt on all sales.

In December 1980, it became known that the deep-freeze rice and deep-freeze vegetable products of Iglo contained nitrite, a carcinogen. At least two people died after eating the contaminated products and many others became ill. Iglo recalled approximately 300 tonnes of deep-freeze products.

Rolls-Royce back to the shop

Not only the food industry, but other sectors too, are susceptible to errors in the production process. Among them, the automotive industry has had many a product recall.

In October 1997, Mercedes-Benz in Sweden conducted test drives with its new Mercedes-Benz A class, a small and practical automobile. The so-called moose test, where a car is tested to see how it copes with a sudden evasive manoeuvre, went completely wrong. The car proved not to be able to hold the road and could overturn. Mercedes was forced to delay the launch of the new vehicle and to re-engineer its set-up.

Even Rolls-Royce and Bentley, the archetypal status vehicles, had to recall more than 1,725 vehicles in October 1999 because they had problems with the thermostats and seat-warming systems. Something similar happened to Ford Europe in December 2000. A bug in the computer chip for the airbag meant that the company had to recall 2,500 Ford Mondeos.

The country is paralysed

People are often the victims of a crisis, but crises are often about people, too. Social conflicts arise for the most diverse reasons and are fought out in the most diverse ways. Personnel express their dissatisfaction through official or wildcat strikes, demonstrations, sit-ins, road blockades, sometimes even with violence, enough to paralyse a company or a whole sector very quickly.

In September 2000, Belgian roads were blockaded by disgruntled truckers. They parked their vehicles on all the important access roads from and to the major cities. Economic life was completely disrupted. Employees had to stay at home for the simple reason that they were unable to get to work. Goods transport was brought to a halt on Belgian roads. Foreign transport companies also experienced major disruptions.

Employees can also take centre stage in a crisis in another way. An epidemic can bring work in a company to a complete halt. At the end of the 1990s, a serious flu epidemic broke out in Scotland and northern England. Thousands of people were so sick that they had to be admitted to hospital. Many patients died. Within no time, clinics were filled beyond capacity. Patients were forced to stay in corridors and improvised rooms were set up in the basements. Many doctors and nurses also contracted the virus. The few doctors who were left standing could no longer deal with the flood of patients. Schools, companies and government were completely paralysed.

The cowboy without a cigarette

If a company's economic activity itself becomes the subject of a crisis, that company has a major problem. It is being hit in the core of its activities. A company that brings a legal product to market in a legal way can nevertheless find itself in difficulties.

The tobacco industry is a prime example of a sector with those types of problems. Tobacco products are freely available for sale in newspaper shops, supermarkets, petrol stations, etc, and still the government considers them to be dangerous products that should be banished as much as possible. The tobacco industry regularly finds its hands tied, for instance by the ban on advertising, which has become increasingly restrictive over the years.

In the first phase, active advertising was prohibited: it was no longer permissible to portray cowboys with a cigarette, either in the hand or hanging casually from the corner of the mouth. Only the product itself could be shown. The result: posters showed packages of cigarettes, but no smokers were anywhere to be seen. In the second phase, the product itself could not be shown. Furthermore, all packages and signage had to carry messages such as 'Smoking damages health' and 'Smoking kills'.

The next step was a complete ban on tobacco advertising. From that point on, placing the name of tobacco products on merchandise was no longer permitted, and that was a red line through the campaigns of the tobacco producers. Through merchandising and sponsoring, they had sought a workaround to escape the strict regulations: Marlboro developed the Marlboro Classics clothing line; Camel started the adventurous Camel Trophy; and Richmond organized vacations. Tobacco manufacturers also sponsored events such as Formula 1 races and rock festivals, on a major scale.

In Belgium, tobacco advertising is only permitted at specific tobacco sales points. Additional restrictive measures were also imposed, such as the prohibition on smoking in public buildings and restaurants. Many private organizations and companies followed the government in taking steps against smoking in their establishments.

A case in point: those who took the train 30 or 40 years ago were forced to search for the non-smoking compartment. Today, in Belgium, you have to look for the 'isolation cell' where smoking is still allowed. Passenger carriers (airlines, railways, subways) in an increasing number of countries have become smoke-free.

The greatest civilian nuclear disaster in history

Environmental contamination, an explosion, a fire, a transport accident in which poisonous substances are released: these are all situations that could lead to an environmental crisis. It could be the result of a wide variety of causes: incomplete safety or security plans, a defective piece of equipment, the human factor. In today's world, environmental protection and a healthy environment in which to live and work are hot topics. It goes without saying that organizations faced with a crisis situation should communicate information quickly and accurately to the population and those in the immediate vicinity.

On 12 December 1999, the Maltese oil tanker *Erika* went aground near the Breton coast. A large oil spill contaminated a stretch of water 400 kilometres long as well as Breton beaches. Fish and birds died in their thousands. The French people were furious.

The nuclear disaster at the Chernobyl power plant on 26 April 1986 is an environmental crisis that will remain etched in the memory for all time. Fire in one of the nuclear reactors caused an extremely high dose of radiation to be released. Whole villages had to be evacuated, thousands of people became ill, many people died. And the Soviet authorities tried to brush the accident under the carpet. Chernobyl grew to become the biggest civilian nuclear disaster in history. In response, many countries tightened up their controls and maintenance procedures on their nuclear reactors.

Criminal intent

Crises are not just the result of accidents, the human factor, natural elements or a tragic confluence of circumstances. Sometimes, criminal intent plays a part. Often, the perpetrators want to make a statement or to force a company or government to agree to certain demands by extortion.

On 19 April 1995, a large bomb exploded in a federal government building in Oklahoma City in the United States. One hundred and sixty-eight people died in the attack and 500 others were wounded. The perpetrator, Timothy McVeigh, called his deed 'a legitimate tactical means' in his personal war against the US government. McVeigh was sentenced to death and was executed on 11 June 2001.

In Belgium, the bloody attacks of the 'Gang of Nijvel' drove the country into crisis during the 1980s. The gang struck several times during the period 1983 to 1985. A total of 28 people died in Belgium as a result of their terrorist attacks on sites such as stores in the Delhaize supermarket chain.

Terrorist attacks are carried out for the most diverse reasons, but there is usually a single common thread: the terrorists want to bring a country, a government, an organization or a company to a state of crisis. Examples are numerous: the bomb that exploded on a Pan American Airlines Boeing 747 above the Scottish town of Lockerbie. The perpetrator was a Libyan terrorist, 270 passengers died. Eleven people died in the poison gas attack by the Japanese Aum Shrinkrikyo sect on the subway in Tokyo. And, of course, the attacks by Al-Qa'ida on the Twin Towers of the World Trade Center in New York and on the Pentagon in Washington, DC. The attacks did not stop there: bombs were carried on to London public transport on 7 July 2005. Fifty-two people died in that attack and nearly 1,000 people were wounded. The four bomb explosions on the commuter trains in Madrid cost 191 people their lives.

Conclusion

Every day, crises, accidents and disasters make the news. Many crises have a high level of tension. Sometimes, they resemble fictional thrillers. They are not detective stories, however. They did not arise from the creative spirit of Sir Arthur Conan Doyle or Agatha Christie. This is the hard reality.

2 Proactive crisis communication planning

Plans are useless, but planning is indispensable…

Nick Leighton (United Arab Emirates) and Tony Shelton (United States)

Introduction

In this chapter you'll discover how preparation is the key to successfully communicating through a crisis situation. While you can't control what the media say and write about the crisis, it is possible – through a proactive crisis communication plan – to limit possible damage and to largely manage the news agenda. We lay out who should be involved, what preparations should be made and how to build the proactive crisis communication plan. With this plan in place, we provide advice on how it can be used to maximum advantage.

> *There's no such thing as bad publicity except your own obituary.*
> Brendan Behan

Don't believe it! If you don't think the media have the ability to pull down, destroy and then regurgitate everything you and your company stand for, then you clearly have not opened a newspaper. Bad news sells. It sells newspapers, TV news airtime and click-throughs on web pages.

If you think the bad publicity will stop because it might cause your organization embarrassment, financial loss or damage your reputation then think again. You need to take control of the situation. You need to protect your image. You need a proactive crisis communication plan.

Need for a plan

Why have a proactive crisis communication plan? Because it can lead to crisis control and control is the name of the game.

The crisis communication mantra is simple – concern, relief and reassurance. But we're getting ahead of ourselves. Let us first look at how we can set up a proactive crisis communication plan.

What is a crisis?

We're not necessarily talking aircraft falling out of the sky or ocean liners hitting icebergs. These are certainly disasters that call for crisis communication, but people's lives do not need to be in danger for there to be a crisis. For the rest of us who have an interest in protecting a professional business reputation, far lesser events can become crises. For example, in a period of three weeks, three clients at Nick Leighton's agency, NettResults, have each had a crisis:

- A new business in the area of media: their very visible general manager quit after one month in the job.
- A real estate developer about to launch: their CEO left and defrauded the company of millions of dollars.
- A technology company: its CEO was questioned by police after the death of an employee, whose remains were found washed up on the local beach.

In none of these three instances had the company or its employees done anything wrong. They had been neither negligent nor unethical. Yet they found their businesses to be at risk if they could not control the message. It wouldn't take anyone working against them (the senior managers who were no longer with our clients were not turning the cogs of the media against our clients) for the situation to get nasty:

- The media business was concerned that employees might leave (as had happened *en masse* to a competitor only a couple of weeks earlier) and general opinion was that the recent launch would not be successful without the flamboyant leader.

- The real estate developer was concerned that the millions of dollars of sales expected in the short term would not be forthcoming, as potential investors believed their money could be defrauded from the company. Besides, who was now heading the company that was to deliver their luxury real estate?
- The technology company was concerned that confidence in its CEO would be damaged, leading to institutions and banks calling back their loans.

Still don't think you need a crisis plan?

Sometimes something happens that has nothing at all to do with your company and still a crisis communication situation arises. NettResults had a client that operated from headquarters in the United Arab Emirates across the Gulf region. A subsidiary company it had sold over three years previously, based in Europe, was being investigated for tax evasion. A journalist investigating the story grabbed at facts that were untrue in order to tie our client's 'newsworthy' name to it. The client had no link to the company in Europe (and hadn't for some time), but the journalist did not look for the correct legal papers that proved disassociation, as it would have lessened the newsworthiness of the story.

Another client of the same agency builds water utility facilities. They built such a facility under contract to a separate organization. After construction was complete and whilst the facility was being managed by its owners, it experienced a 'fault' that caused a sewage leak. This leak had nothing to do with the construction of the facility, but once the word got out, the press got hold of it and sought to apportion blame.

If you do not have a quick and effective crisis communication plan in place, the press will fill that 'media vacuum' with information, comment or opinion, which does more to sell their story and less to protect your business. *Still don't think you need a crisis plan?*

All right. What if one of your top employees were to be accused of a crime that is of a personal nature and has nothing to do with your organization? Does the organization still have to comment? Most likely, yes.

Officials at NASA, the US space agency, found themselves in the midst of a crisis they could never have imagined when astronaut Lisa Nowak was arrested and charged with attempting to murder her reputed romantic rival for the affections of another astronaut. To the media, it did not matter that the crime had nothing to do with sending people into space. The backlash from the story immediately threatened the agency's reputation and NASA leaders soon decided they would have to comment or they would be able to exert no control over the story. They adapted the communication approach they had used successfully in operational crises to a crisis that was definitely not NASA-like.

How did they do so? At the time of writing, excluding a few awkward word choices at a news conference, NASA had done a good job with its communication. For instance, the director of NASA's Johnson Space Center, where the astronauts train, hit exactly the right tone. In a statement, he noted that Astronaut Nowak was officially on a 30-day leave and had 'been removed from flight status and related activities. We will continue to monitor developments in the case'.

Just the facts. The statement was neutral, covered the essential elements, and included no unintended references to whether the astronaut was guilty of the charges – or whether the alleged incident had even occurred. That neutral expression of the facts is especially necessary when you are talking about something as important as an alleged criminal act. (At the end of Nowak's 30-day leave, NASA dismissed her from the astronaut programme, undoubtedly, at least in part, due to the unrelenting media attention.)

Corporations could learn much from the NASA official's early, simple statement. If it's your crisis, you have to say something, but keep it neutral. To make sure you don't stray from the facts, write down your statement and read it word for word.

Is there any way your business might not be able to deliver the product or service that you make your money from? Is there any reason why your top management might leave? Is there a reason why lots of staff might walk out together? Is there anything in the world that could possibly lead to customers not being able to purchase or take delivery of your product or service? Is it conceivable that any of your offices or facilities could suffer damage or loss? Is it possible that someone in your company could say something in a public place that is misconstrued as dishonest, unethical, biased or derogatory in any way? Are you 100 per cent sure your taxes have been filed correctly? Are there no skeletons in the closet? Have you, and all your management team and all your investors lived a pure and 100 per cent honest existence? Has every one of your clients lived a pure and 100 per cent honest existence? Is there just a chance that something, somewhere, sometime could be bad for your organization?

Still don't think you need a crisis plan? Then read Chapters 4, 5, 6, 7, 8, 12 and 13 in this book. In these chapters, you'll not only see examples of common crises, but you will also find out what is so unique about them and how to deal with them.

You *do* need a crisis plan.

What a crisis plan provides

When you find yourself in a crisis communication situation you have one goal: to protect the reputation of the organization by:

- communicating the right message;
- at the right time;
- to the right people.

Responding quickly and with confidence is the only way your organization can seize control of the crisis communication and turn it to your advantage. Look on it as a wise investment.

Elements of a plan

What you're developing is quite simple, really. To have a clear and concise, proactive crisis communication plan you need guidelines for:

- the right message;
- to whom that message should be told;
- who should tell it;
- the right time to tell it.

As part of that plan, you also need to understand how you will communicate internally and agree on the above elements as quickly as possible, ensuring that everyone within your organization has the correct authority and sign-off.

People

Selecting a team

Let's get a crisis team together.

This is nothing like being the person in your department who gets an extra bonus for being 'first aid' trained. Your crisis team needs to be small, agile, alert and reachable. A team that needs to have absolute authority and won't be afraid to tell other board members what to do.

When an agency is called into a client to construct a proactive crisis communication plan, the first meeting ideally should be at the next company-wide board level meeting. The crisis professionals have to be in front of all the C-level executives who could in the future be a part of the crisis and its success. Everyone has to be on board with the idea that a plan is going to be put in place and that they will not have a problem abiding by it.

This is not easy. Let's not even try to pretend it is. In this situation, the crisis advisers normally must highlight to the board:

- what PR is, and how it differs from advertising;
- what a crisis is;
- what possible crises could happen to the company;
- how that might appear to the press and what the media might write/air;
- the bottom-line cost to the organization;
- the long-term damage it could do to the organization;
- that there is a solution that can save/make the company lots of money;
- that, if all agree that time, effort and money will be put into making a proactive crisis communication plan, then it is only going to work in practice if everyone abides by it.

Who do you want on your team? You will need:

- At least two spokespeople; you need back-up.
- The CEO, owner or ultimate stakeholder: basically, someone who, with guidance, will make the calls and define the actions (and ideally someone who does not report to anyone else when not in a crisis situation).
- Your lead in-house communication professional.
- Your full PR agency team: for breadth of reach and redundancy reasons – with one key contact point (normally your account manager).

Who do you not want on a crisis communication team? Your accountant and your attorney. That is not to say they do not have valuable roles to play.

Let's look at the role of the accountant first. That person needs to be working with the operational responders, when there is a crisis that threatens property, for instance, to make sure those people have access to the funding they need to bring in adequate resources without delay.

And the attorney: we have found that the best time to bring in the attorney is in the planning stage of the crisis communication plan. Help that person realize that both the attorney and the communicator have the same goal – to protect the reputation of the organization. Have the attorney review the plan in progress. Have the attorney sign off in advance on the kinds of information that can be released and even the template for your future crisis statements (see page 42).

Then, in the midst of the crisis – even if the lead decision maker insists on an opinion from the attorney – there is a much greater chance that communication will still proceed. Exclude the attorney from the planning at your peril. Too many companies have suffered damage to their image simply because the attorney was consulted only at the last minute and then convinced the CEO that 'it's too risky to say anything right now'.

Remember this: if there is someone in the organization who can potentially shut down essential communication during a crisis, bring them into the planning stage. Making them a part of the process will pay big dividends later on.

Team roles and responsibilities

Each member of the team needs to have a function in a crisis. We need a mouth, a brain and hands.

The mouth – spokespeople

You need to have a minimum of two spokespeople – and you may need more. This depends on how broad your organization is and in how many geographical markets you are present. A company based in one geographical location that manufactures one product will probably be fine with just two spokespeople. If you operate on different continents, you'll probably, for reasons of cultural understanding and time differences, need more.

Spokesperson 1 – the primary, number one spokesperson representing the organization.

Spokesperson 2 – the second person if number 1 is not available or if spokespeople are required in multiple locations.

If your business sensibly needs a third and fourth spokesperson, then designate them.

Spokespeople alone do not decide what is to be said. They are the 'mouth' of the organization. Ideally they are professional, presentable, corporate and trained in how to be in front of a camera and deal with the press. Often we find that CEOs are reluctant to give up this position to others, but they should be honest with themselves. If they are not the absolute right person for the job, then it should go to someone who is better suited.

If the CEO is not normally the spokesperson *outside* a crisis, then he or she is probably not the right person *in* a crisis. Let us not forget that whoever is the standard spokesperson for a company will have an existing relationship with the press. That relationship can be invaluable in a crisis.

Multifaceted organizations that find themselves in complex crisis situations may need *specialist spokespeople*. These are in-house senior managers who are normally highly specialized. For example, if an engineering and construction company also has in-house architects, one might be needed to explain a complex situation.

Specialist spokespeople are not normally needed to deal with the crisis, but may be needed to add credibility and explain 'the way it is' if a crisis relates to an area that is outside regular news reader/viewers' daily comprehension. If you do not provide your own specialist, you can bet that the news publications and stations will – and from that point you start to lose control.

All spokespeople need to be media trained. See Chapter 10 for more details on media training.

The brain – the crisis committee

The committee is led by one team leader (often the CEO of the company) and also comprises the other crisis team members. The brain probably does not include specialist spokespeople.

Ideally, you'll want three to five people to act as the brain. Irrespective of whether you have an odd or even number of people in the team, you need to define whether your team leader has a deciding vote (a vote given to the committee leader to resolve a deadlock and which can be exercised only when such a deadlock exists).

The crisis committee's first job is to decide how they will operate. The simplest way is that the committee must be in a majority agreement for all actions. However, this might not be the optimal approach. As Margaret Thatcher (ex British Prime Minister) said, 'consensus is the negation of leadership'. We can tell you from our experience, if the leader is ready to lead, and the others in the team are also on board with this manner of decision making, then this is the most effective and efficient manner in which to operate during a crisis. You decide what works best for your brain.

The hands – the doers

In a crisis, for control to be seized and then kept, you need to work faster than anyone else does. Division of labour is going to make your crisis control quick and efficient, but only if there is true division and you're not falling over each other.

Communications point

One person has to be the centre for all communications. This person is responsible for:

- getting the committee mobilized;
- communicating the needs of the committee to the mouth (spokespeople) and the other hands;
- approving all communication messages before they go live;
- reporting the situation as it develops to the crisis committee;
- reporting the total crisis once it's all over.

The communications point is normally the lead in-house communications professional.

Media contact team

Reaching the media is often a time-consuming activity. Getting an e-mail off to people on a list is one thing, but following up by phone or in person is something else. If a press conference is going to be called, then this will also be time-consuming.

> NettResults, the firm of author Nick Leighton, operates throughout the Middle East region – with a large expatriate community, and both Arabic and English language publications. We must have a team from at least three ethnic backgrounds to have the language skills, cultural understanding and deep media contacts that will be necessary to get news out quickly and efficiently.

The press contact team will need to:

- have good press contacts;
- have a clean and updated full media list at any given time;
- understand how journalists and editors from different news media work;
- be practised at producing media tools;
- have facilities to translate documents and provide simultaneous translations at a press conference or media interview, if required;
- have the ability to move very quickly.

Note: there may be a need to post news on the company website, so the press contact team also need to have contact with the webmaster for the organization.

The job of press contact normally falls to a public relations agency that has crisis communication experience, but can of course be handled in house if the team members have the necessary strengths and experience.

The plan

It's all in the planning

Now that we have a crisis team ready, we need to do the groundwork. This is the hard work that is needed to make crisis communication successful.

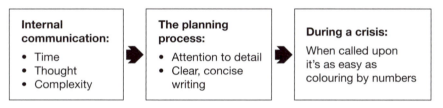

Figure 2.1 Groundwork for the crisis team

Internal communication rules

The name of the game is control, and that can only happen if there is open communication among the team members. In today's business environment this should not be too hard. Every member of the team probably already has a mobile phone and individual e-mail address. If they operate outside a mobile network range for long periods of time, then they probably have a satellite phone. If they don't – make it happen. You can only control a crisis if you can all communicate.

More communication notes – call centres

Because we run a number of crisis communication programmes from an agency point of view, we have made it even easier to communicate. One 24-hour call centre number will reach each and every member of our team. A real person answers the phone (voice mail is not your friend in a crisis) in our call centre and then patches the call to the team member, who can be at his desk, in another NettResults office, on his mobile or wherever he may be. Our call centre is trained to understand how important reaching the right person is during a crisis. It is our personal responsibility to make it happen quickly and efficiently whatever time of day or night. (Nick Leighton)

Also, take a look at 24-hour call centres your client may already be using for another purpose. One of Shelton & Caudle's industrial clients had an existing call centre for pipeline incidents. We trained its operators in what information to collect when someone called in about a crisis and whom to call in company headquarters with that information. Then each employee was given a wallet card with the instructions and number on it. (Tony Shelton)

1. Crisis directory

Quite simple; list the contact points:

First Name:

Last Name:

Position in Organization:

Position in Crisis Team:

Spokesperson:

Office/Direct Phone Number (and extension):

Mobile Number:

Home Number:

E-mail Address:

Contact Notes:

Casting Vote:

Does this person need to approve official communications?

More communication notes – being unavailable

In many cultures, you'll find members of the crisis team who put themselves into circumstances where they are not reachable. Whether that is a round of golf, surfing, skiing, being on a plane or going to the opera, all team members have to be aware of it. If your favourite pastime does not allow for easy communication, then make sure your team know this and document when you are likely to be out of touch and for how long, allowing the team to move forward with the plan without your participation if they cannot reach you.

When you have a crisis directory, in theory anyone can pick it up and communicate effectively with the team. Send each member a soft and hard copy.

More communication notes – letting everyone be 'in the know'

While not everyone in the organization will be in the crisis team, it is a good idea to let everyone, or everyone who matters, know what to do when a crisis occurs. If your organization provides employee handbooks, then the handbook should emphasize that unauthorized press communications are forbidden and list contact information for the 'communication point' in your crisis team for referral if a reporter calls.

If your company has office managers or front reception secretaries, these key people should also be informed who the 'communication point' in your crisis team is. For smaller offices where an office manager keeps a telephone directory of staff members or similar, it would be sensible to log the crisis directory with them.

2. Communication flow

Everyone in the team should be aware of the communication flow in a crisis situation. It should be agreed and then written down and placed in the crisis communication plan. The flow is as follows, and is shown in Figure 2.2:

a. A crisis is identified and brought to the attention of the crisis communication point person.
b. The point person informs or brings together the complete crisis committee.
c. While the crisis committee is in discussion, the communication point should inform the press contact team in case they are needed (at this point the information dispersed may be on a 'need to know' basis and may just be an alert that their time could be needed).
d. The crisis committee communicates the plan of action to the communication point.
e. The communication point briefs the press contact team and the spokespeople.

Figure 2.2 Communication flow

More communication notes – getting together

If the crisis team members are not located in the same place then there may be a need for more sophisticated communication than all walking into the same office. More critically, the crisis committee (the brain) needs to be in a situation in which they can discuss the crisis and the suitable communication. If dispersed and your office phones do not support conference calls (or if there is a chance that no one will be in the office at a time that a crisis hits) you might want to prepare a conference-call facility. There are a number that are secure and free to use on the web. The crisis communication point is responsible for carrying out the research in the planning stage in case it is called upon.

Once a crisis communication situation is in progress, all communication flows to and from the communication point. The communication point uses the spokespeople and the press contact team as the conduit to the press and thus to all stakeholders.

3. Keeping track of the press

Internally, when it comes to a crisis situation, contact with the press needs to be measured and recorded. It pays to have a press contact sheet ready for use once a crisis hits. Just like a crisis directory, this is a simple form, but will be worth its preparation before the crisis.

More communication notes – press contact sheet

Time: .....:..... am/pm

Mon Tue Wed Thu Fri Sat Sun

Date: ....

Name of caller: ....

Publication: ....

Media organization: ....

Media contact's deadline: ....

Preferred contact method: ....

Telephone number: ....

Mobile number: ....

E-mail: ....

Question/s asked: ....

....

....

....

Person who dealt with enquiry: ....

Information provided: ....

....

....

Person who approved (if required): ....

Follow up (if any): ....

Target, tools, message, timing

Before we look at the targets, tools, message and timing in a crisis, we need to understand that there should be an ongoing media relations plan in place. This communication plan should identify the basics needed when dealing with the press. This will provide the background that is necessary for all members of the crisis communication team to be on the same page.

This seems obvious, but in our experience even clients who have been successfully communicating with the press for a number of years rarely have the basics written down and agreed to by the executives in the company. If this is the case, then Appendix 1 (see page 207) shows a basic sheet that can be worked through in under an hour (getting everyone to agree may take longer) and will provide the necessary factual information for both a crisis plan and also ongoing proactive media relations.

With an understanding of the company's basic facts, the crisis team needs to develop a messaging document and agree upon it. This messaging document has three stages to it:

1. By looking at various areas of the business, we can identify core messages to be used with the media pre-crisis.
2. Following from that, it is easier to anticipate situations that may go against the main messaging, and then clearly identify how the organization should respond.
3. We can now identify questions that the media may ask of the organization and then develop standard answers.

A suggested work plan can be seen in Appendix 2 (see page 210).

Target

Who are the stakeholders of your organization? Basically, when you find yourself in a crisis, who will it affect? We identify these groups now because, 1) we don't want to forget a group in the heat of the moment, and 2) the better we can target groups of people, the better we can target the correct press to communicate with them.

Most usually, an organization will want to take care of the following people:

- employees;
- customers;
- prospective customers;
- suppliers;
- investors (both private and institutional);
- community members.

If your company is publicly held, then there will be a number of other stakeholders – some of these are identified further in Chapter 5 where we take a closer look at financial issues.

More communication notes – who are your customers?

Be conscious of who your customers are. Most companies sell through a channel of some kind: a property developer sells through real estate agents; a computer company may have distributors and resellers. You need to be aware of all channel partners because each will have their dedicated media and messages will eventually have to be tailored for each target.

Once you have a list of your targets, you need to pass this to your press contact team. They need to draw up a list of all media within each group. There will be multiple media types (newspapers, trade publications, TV, etc) and cross-over (same media for multiple groups – often with a different contact point, for example, both the business and local news editors of a newspaper).

It is now the job of the press contact team to prioritize this list. In the midst of crisis communication, whilst it may be possible to send a news release to everyone on a list, it may only be possible to speak to the most important by phone. Prioritization will be a factor of:

- reach (number of people the media reach);
- speed of broadcast (web pages are often posted within minutes, a TV station in a matter of hours; obviously a daily newspaper will be slower, and a monthly trade title slower yet);
- importance (some titles are considered more important than others – that's just the way it is);
- existing relationship with the media (if you have a good long-term relationship with an editor, you had better keep him or her updated if you want to continue the good relationship through the crisis and beyond).

Tools

For each target that has been identified above, your press contact team will be able to draw up a full contact list – office phone numbers (with extensions or direct numbers), mobile phone numbers, e-mail, fax, etc. As with regular media relations, each press member has a preferred method of communication (this should be noted).

You should also be aware of what type of information they will want to receive. A newspaper, for example, will want to have still images.

Again, it is a 'vacuum game': if you do not provide an image, they may search for one, and it might not be the one you would have chosen. High-resolution images of your company, your spokespeople and, if possible, lifestyle images (people interacting with your products) should all be on file and ready to use. When dealing with TV, you'll want to have b-roll ready, too.

Remember, you're going to be short of time during a crisis, so you might like to consider having high-resolution images and b-roll uploaded to an FTP server or some other equivalent. That way you only need to point your press contacts to the right place and material will be streaming into their news reports.

Message

By developing your company media relations messaging document and having standard company information available (see Appendices 1 and 2) you can forecast possible crisis scenarios and what a response might be. While this process is based on the media relations of a company, the advantage is that you may identify potential crises that are preventable and thus modify existing methods of operation.

This is the most proactive part of the proactive crisis communications plan. Anticipating crises allows you to produce game plans and suggested communication messages before the event. Appendix 3 shows how you might be able to anticipate crises (see page 213).

One-off communication will not solve a crisis. For a large-scale crisis you need to develop your message over a number of different communication pieces and try to steer the following path: concern, relief and reassurance.

First of all, you need to show *concern* and consideration for what happened. You have to be honest and open that a crisis has occurred and that as an organization you are doing everything in your power to find out exactly what happened and how it happened.

Next, you need to subtly express *relief*. This is where you will probably demonstrate some internal company safeguards, showing that your company actually had the crisis under control well before it got out of hand.

Third, you need to show *reassurance* that all possible steps are being taken to right the wrong and to make adjustments to keep the event from happening again. You have to show that you are learning from your mistakes.

How to deal with reporters is further discussed in the media training chapter – Chapter 10 – but for the process of developing your message you will find the pointers in Appendix 4 to be most useful (see page 216). As you identify situations, you'll quickly find out that these will not be completely developed messages. You'll need to wait until you are in the crisis situation before that can be done, but this process will allow you to be ready.

You may be able to develop holding statements. Holding statements are pre-prepared short messages that can be used in a crisis to indicate to the media that you are taking the crisis seriously. They are ideal for filling the 'media vacuum'. Bear in mind that one of the worst things that a company can be quoted as saying is, 'No comment.' A holding statement allows you to fill the vacuum and gives you time to prepare your full messages.

Sample holding statement A

A ___ [the crisis] at ___ [location] involving ___[company and possibly names] occurred today at ___ [time and date]. The incident is under investigation and more information will be forthcoming.

For more information as it become available please contact: [press contact team]

For more information about ___ [company name] please visit: _____ [web address].

Sample holding statement B (when you have more information)

At _____ [time/day], there was a/we were informed of_____ [the crisis] at _____[facility/location]. No one/_____ [number of persons] has/have been reported to be injured. We have taken a number of actions:

_____

The cause of the _____ [crisis] is under investigation and we expect to have more information later. For more information, please contact: _____ [name/department]. For more information about _____ [company name], please visit _____ [web address].

Timing

To gain control of the flow of information, you'll need to work very, very quickly. If you do not, you can expect the press to move before you do, and then you lose control as they start to shape and tell the story. The best way to work quickly is to have a proactive crisis communication plan in place. If you take preventive measures and prepare as best you can, you can get through a crisis communication situation, perhaps even with better media coverage and stronger press contacts than before the crisis hit.

Conclusion

The name of the game is control. Your proactive crisis communication plan is developed to protect the reputation of your organization by communicating the right message, at the right time, to the right people. If you don't seize control of the situation there will be an information vacuum that will be filled by the media as they feel fit – often to the detriment of your organization.

First, select the right crisis team. There has to be a mouth, a brain and hands to your crisis team, allowing you to think clearly, communicate effectively and act quickly.

Next, determine the internal communication rules – this is how the organization will communicate within itself during a crisis. A crisis directory is set up, the communication flow is defined and we set up templates to record and keep track of media enquiries.

Then prepare the proactive crisis communication plan with four distinct areas. You should define the various targets with whom you may need to communicate. You have to develop ready-made tools that are easy to pick up in a crisis situation. The possible messages that are pre-approved to use in a crisis communication should be thought about, developed and approved. Lastly, take note of how quickly you can move in a crisis situation and further develop the plan so the organization can move as quickly as possible.

3 Image as a part of corporate strategy

Building reputation for long-term benefit

Tom Gable (United States)

Introduction

The major national media regularly rank the most admired corporations in the United States, listing the core values that helped them gain fame. Is the effort just the business equivalent of selecting the most popular in the high school yearbook? Or should companies and organizations concern themselves with image and reputation?

Definitely the latter. According to studies over almost two decades by Charles Fombrun (author of *Reputation* and *Fame and Fortune*) and others, intangible assets such as reputation may provide companies with a more enduring source of competitive advantage than patents, innovative design, clever marketing and proprietary technologies. But reputation is neither hyperbole nor what political commentators refer to as 'spin' (where the strategy is to interpret or manipulate a statement or event from a particular viewpoint, especially in a way meant to sway public opinion and, in the case of a crisis, forestall or mitigate negative publicity).

Companies can't simply claim leadership, operating superiority, dedication to world-class service or other attributes in their marketing and PR copy. They must build image into their corporate strategy, then develop the culture and operating practices that bring the reputation to life for all their target audiences. They must be prepared to 'walk the talk' over time, turning the name and brand into a valuable asset with everyone it touches.

The results? Fombrun provides convincing evidence on how reputation can have a positive impact on growth versus peers in profit margin, employee morale, community goodwill, investor support, relationships with vendors and suppliers and overall organizational pride. He calls it 'reputational capital'.

Reputations add value over time

Reputations support growth on the way up and also help deflect or minimize negative events or attacks. Organizations with a good reputation, impeccable history of positive contributions to the community and leaders who walk the talk in all that they do are given the benefit of the doubt in negative situations. Their values and history are known and appreciated. A crisis, then, becomes a one-off situation that its many publics know the organization will quickly resolve. Stock prices take minimal hits. Lost sales rebound quickly. The organization manages the crisis to further demonstrate its core values. New stories become part of the corporate lore.

Studies over nearly 20 years show that intangible assets such as reputation may well provide companies with a more enduring source of competitive advantage than its patents and technologies. It speeds growth on the way up and protects against crises or criticism. But short-term initiatives or those based on insufficient or misleading information don't work. Achieving the desired position and strong reputation requires investing in your image over time and providing ongoing proof of principle – walking the talk.

To quote Charles Fombrun from his book *Reputation*, 'achieving prestige requires a long-term outlook toward building competitive advantage'. Companies develop winning reputations by both creating and projecting a set of skills that their constituents recognize as unique. 'Achieving uniqueness requires routine actions that demonstrate credibility and earn the trust of key constituents,' Fombrun notes. Studies by Fombrun and others show that the most respected companies built their reputations by developing practices that integrated economic and social considerations into their competitive strategies. 'They not only do things right,' to quote Fombrun, 'they do the right things.' Their name becomes a valuable asset.

Determining how you want to be known

A reputation develops from a company's uniqueness and identity-shaping practices that over time lead constituents to perceive the company as credible, reliable, trustworthy, and responsible. Deeper yet, they walk their talk.

Companies, organizations and institutions need to become strategic and visionary about how they want to be known one, two and three years from now and beyond. To get there, determine which first words you would like to have pop up in the frontal lobe of any constituent when they hear your name – the evocative thought. This includes people inside and outside the company. If you have a clear idea of how you want to be known, you have a great start. If not, you need to conduct extensive competitive research and develop a candid assessment of your strengths and weaknesses and whether or not you can be clearly differentiated.

Determine how you want to be known and then build the strategic roadmap to get there. Do you have core values that separate you from the herd? Have you supported important community causes for long periods of time? Are your people active in non-profit organizations and respected for their contributions, not just lending their name to the letterhead?

Establishing competitive advantage

What you stand for can be a true differentiator. If you stand for the highest ethical standards in your profession, that's important. Then, can you demonstrate it over time? What will the proof of principle – the evidence – look like?

Do you have a real competitive advantage with your technology or do your products stand apart from others in a particular niche? Can you truly be identified as a leader of a category or niche? If not, think about your 'magic' and proprietary processes. Can you create the impression of having a magical black box inside your organization that helps you deliver better services and results than your competitors? What is your secret ingredient that no one else has? Can you make tangible the intangibles?

Core values are what you stand for – the differentiating elements that help you stand out, build reputation and gain respect. Focus on three or four core values as the pillars of your reputation.

Communicating what you stand for

Here's an example from a complex assignment during media training with different members of the oncology team at Pfizer. Their mission is to be a world leader in developing new medicines for the treatment of cancers where patients are without treatment or have limited or diminishing options.

The following three core values emerged from several hours of brainstorming and analysis:

1. Pfizer is committing US $7.5 billion a year to pursue new medicines – a level unmatched in the industry.
2. Pfizer has assembled the best and the brightest cancer scientists from around the globe – a United Nations of recognized leaders in drug discovery and development.
3. Pfizer scientists are committed to success, often pursuing cures for a decade or more until they find the one success out of a thousand promising compounds.

From those core values, the scientists had impressive research projects in the pipeline that would provide positive supporting evidence. For example, in the US $7.5 billion core value, they can add how much it costs to develop a drug, the rate of failure, the need for new technology to speed the discovery process and other details on cost of equipment, etc. In 2, they can refer to published works of their scientific teams and successful new products. In 3, they can give personal anecdotes, such as one scientist who started pursuing a new compound to treat cancer when his first daughter was born. That same compound is now entering Phase III (the last stage of clinical trials before applying to the Federal Drug Administration for approval) as his daughter enters middle school! The scientists also talked about getting up early or staying up late for teleconference sessions with colleagues around the globe, or travelling inordinately to meet and advance the science.

Core values are the foundation for benefits that are delivered to your different constituencies. They are the major ingredients of success. General Electric wants to be number one or two in each market it serves because of its culture of innovation, customer focus and ability to deliver the highest quality on a consistent basis, using its internal process called Six Sigma. From those three pillars of the image, GE provides ongoing evidence for each core value. It introduces new products. It upgrades existing ones and replaces defective products. It also promotes its Six Sigma process to other companies as a means of raising their standards. GE is a guru. More GE alumni run major corporations than those from any other Fortune 100 firm.

Planning to reach all potential audiences

GE and many like it have strategic plans to communicate with their many constituencies over time. They understand the various channels of communication in the PR world. As noted by Al Ries in his many books, PR comes first, followed by advertising and other activities. We come to judge companies by what we hear from trusted sources – the media, peers, informal and formal networks, and influential leaders through the community, an industry or a region.

Michael Porter of Harvard, in his landmark book, *Competitive Advantage,* talked about differentiating along the entire chain of value a company or organization provides to its many constituents. He shows how to examine every link in a chain. Which attributes of each can demonstrate value and help you stand out from the competition? If quality is your differentiator, how does that play in each link? Do you have the best outside suppliers? Do you have the best manufacturing processes, the best customer service, and the best logistics? This creates great PR opportunities. You can promote the quality of each link and its accomplishments. Then, wherever people turn, they are seeing evidence of your reputation as it grows.

Fombrun says PR efforts should be invested in building long-term behavioural relationships with strategic publics – those that affect the ability of the organization to accomplish its mission. His studies, 10 years after the Porter book, provide validation for launching a systematic effort to reach customers, investors, employees, regulators, the local and wider community, suppliers and providers with compelling evidence to support your core values.

Turning vision into reality

Once you've determined how you want to be known, you need to be consistent, continuous and creative. Image becomes a part of your corporate strategy. You examine every channel of communication and opportunity, then plot your plan over time on a project management spreadsheet to build image and reputation as you would a great skyscraper: the big vision and then all the activities and components necessary to bring the vision to reality. Promote your core values. You don't just send things out to different targets: you build relationships. You provide ongoing proof of principle. And you have a personality. In working with everything from start-ups in biotech and internet payment systems to a Fortune 100 company, we have found that positive personalities can help further differentiate a company and its products or services.

This isn't an ego trip for the CEO, generating media clips to show the grandchildren. It's about being human, telling stories, and bringing an organization to life in new and creative ways. Culture can be another differentiator. Is it collegial, innovative and quirky in a positive way? The heart and soul of an organization can become a powerful differentiator. The people bringing these attributes to life among multiple constituencies become ambassadors to further build the organization's reputation and long-term relationships.

Tell real stories

In his book, *Body of Truth,* Dan Hill provides evidence that telling real stories with passion and personality can help to differentiate an organization. Stories – real stories – add depth to reputations and connect with audiences. Think about mining your organization for stories that illustrate the desired reputation. Gather the information and then share it. Celebrate behaviours. Nordstrom, the department store chain in the United States, prides itself on customer service, empowers its employees to go to extraordinary lengths to provide the service and then celebrates the best examples of the culture at work. These stories provide ongoing evidence to support its reputation and become part of the corporate fabric.

PR drives it. As Al and Laura Ries discussed in their book, *The Fall of Advertising and the Rise of PR,* PR leads in brand development and reputation management. It lights the fire. Advertising and other disciplines fan the flames. With media and research databases that retain information to perpetuity, the ease and power of searching for information on the internet and newly ingrained habits of searching for information first before acting, positive PR can take on a life of its own. With the databases of the world filled with positive information about your organization, its people and deeds, a crisis may be viewed as just a slight blemish on an otherwise perfect subject. Your organization has proven itself over time. Evidence abounds. What is the source of the aberration? Is it a one-off occurrence? Happenstance? An attack by a gadfly with questionable motives?

Appeal to higher standards, bigger ideas

In an engagement with one of the region's largest real estate developers, Gable PR developed a two-year programme to support the approval of a master plan for a 14,000-acre development that would be home to 40,000 residents. It would feature new schools, a shopping centre, bike and hiking trails, and a mix of housing from lower-cost apartments to executive homes on large lots. The agency positioned the project as the ultimate smart plan and the perfect future home for upscale families. Strategies included community relations, building coalitions, media relations, crisis communications, public affairs and other activities. The client was dedicated to making its plan a new standard for community development. For every component of the project, it retained the most respected consultants and charged them with setting their own high standards, from roads and infrastructure, to landscaping, aesthetics and down to the most elaborate drainage plan ever developed to deal with run-off water during rain storms to protect the environment and neighbouring communities.

Community planners, architects, engineers and economists met with community planning groups and the media long before major milestones would occur in the approval process. When critics began holding meetings and protesting against the development, their motives (largely no-growth advocates) immediately came into question. Outrageous claims were made and quickly countered. The critics lost their credibility in the community and with the media. The bottom-line result: unanimous approval by the City and the development of what would ultimately become the most successful development in the history of the company.

How can any organization build reputation for the long term? Based on extensive, ongoing research and experience working for a wide range of clients for more than three decades, eight key areas emerged that provide a foundation any company can use to incorporate image as a part of its corporate strategy.

1. Analyse the competition

How do you want to be known over the next two to three years? What do you stand for? Do you own a category or niche? Do you have competitive advantages? Can you clearly differentiate yourself from the competition?

For a quick exercise, Gable PR recommends creating a matrix. List yourself and your competitors across the top of consecutive columns in an Excel spreadsheet or Word table. Then, in separate boxes below the names, put in each organization's tag line, descriptive clauses (usually found in the first paragraph of a news release), news release boiler-plate language (the 'about' paragraph in a release) and key words or positioning statements. Does everyone sound alike? Do they claim leadership? Do they provide proof? Can any of the claims be substanti-ated? What's there? More important, what's not there?

Use this to start brainstorming on your points of differentiation. For added entertainment, hide the names at the top, pass out the matrix to your colleagues and see how many of the organizations can be identi-fied. (We created an 11-column matrix for a technology client and the CEO could only identify his own company, which sounded particularly daft versus some of the others. A residential real estate developer given a similar challenge identified two out of eight – his development and an evil competitor's in the same geographic area.)

2. Establish core values, positioning

Core values are what an organization stands for – its differentiating elements. Focus on three to four essential core elements (culture of the highest integrity, quality construction or production, technological innovation, shareholder return, giving back to the community, etc) based on your true beliefs, first, and their importance to your different constituencies. These become the pillars of your image and reputa-tion. Then, candidly assess whether you can provide supporting evi-dence for these core values and be able to walk the talk over time. If the answer is yes, press on. If not, re-evaluate.

3. Target external audiences

Make a list of your multiple target audiences and think about how each receives its information and the most influential channels of communi-cation. This will be important in building a strategic plan to reach each constituency, not just with compelling messages but with actions that support your position.

4. Create a compelling vision, evocative messages

How do you communicate with each constituency and build image and relationships in the process?

From the core values and targeting, determine how you want to be known with each and then begin creating the foundation for an inte-grated messaging strategy. Most organizations waste a lot of time talking to themselves and creating vision and mission statements that appeal to internal audiences. To test your statement, read it to a couple of business acquaintances or outside advisers. If you get dead silence, quizzical expressions or howls of laughter, go back to the drawing board.

For external audiences, create a 30- to 60-second elevator pitch. Imagine you are in an elevator with a potential investor, editor, customer or politician you want to influence. Can you deliver a compelling message? Assume a short building. Summarize vision, position, points of differentiation, where the market is going, why you are wonderful and next steps.

Then, delve into the company lore to find real stories that bring your vision, position and core values to life. According to Dan Hill in his book *Body of Truth,* good stories connect with your audiences and enhance corporate branding. Companies build an emotional aura around themselves, Hill notes, and 'by going deeper and wider, a company can hold off the competition and get closer to consumers'. Companies need to provide perceptual imagery, sensory clues – means of creating emotional links that wouldn't otherwise survive rational scrutiny, according to Hill.

These key ideas need to be woven into the organizational fabric and shared internally before launching future communications into all channels, with ongoing stories demonstrating your values.

5. Assemble the tactical tool kit

Programmes need to be segmented to hit each channel and then implemented with the specific tools best suited to driving results. These can include internal relations and communication, media relations, special events, trade shows and conference programmes, cause marketing, direct marketing, e-mail marketing, advertising, websites, collateral material, guerrilla marketing and other tactics. To reach narrow segments usually requires more direct, personal approaches, while consumers and investors can be influenced best through media relations. Develop a crisis communication plan and have your special crisis website developed but hidden and ready to launch in case a crisis should occur.

6. Draw the strategic road map

Building an image doesn't just happen. It requires a disciplined approach similar to building a great skyscraper or an award-winning new community. Are there key company and industry milestones and other proofs of principle you can roll out strategically, such as new product launches, media or analyst tours, grand openings, analyst reports, published studies, sales milestones, corporate milestones, presentations to major conferences, etc?

When looked at the macro-level, these individual elements can be used to create significant image momentum. Orchestrate the tactical elements to leverage one activity or milestone against others, such as using positive media relations to impact analyst relations, or analyst relations to impact shareholder relations. Time these activities in advance of a major trade show and determine how to involve strategic partners or others to help build the image, or schedule advertising, direct marketing and e-mail marketing to impact just after a media relations blitz.

7. Dare to be measured

Establish key metrics to measure how the image builds over time. These include quantitative, such as output (increased contacts, numbers of releases, speeches, meetings, hits to the website and so on versus historical patterns; calls to free telephone numbers, increased e-mail requests for information, increased daily stock volume, etc). Also measure the qualitative (is the image moving in the desired direction?)

Another consideration is share of voice. Are you rising above the competition in amount of positive coverage? This needs to be analysed in terms of budgets, output and results. Some companies with huge budgets spam the world with news releases yet end up with little share of voice because the messages don't get through. With creative thinking, walking the talk, telling good stories and pursuing a policy of hype-free communication, you can rise above the clutter and cacophony.

8. Ongoing reality checks

I mention 'hype-free' for a reason. Research on news releases issued over Business Wire and PR Newswire in a one-week period revealed that more than half of all companies claimed to be a leader in their industry. Few provided validation. A significant number inflated the news with pompous, self-serving quotes, which the media refer to as 'Lame Ass Quotes', or LAQs.

Organizations need to conduct ongoing reality checks of their messaging to make sure they are communicating with their different constituents, not just themselves. Another test: are you stuck in jargon land? How do your messages compare with respected competitors or companies you admire in other niches? Do the core values and central themes come through in all that you do? Or are you just adding to the LAQ volume?

Conclusion

Incorporating image as a part of corporate strategy and investing in reputation management require a diligent, strategic approach. The approach needs to be creative, consistent, targeted and factual and must support an organization's long-term business and marketing plans. Investing in a quality image and the steps it takes to get there has been proven to provide an ongoing return that organizations can measure in many ways, from internal pride to the bottom line (maybe even reaching the top of a few lists of the most admired and successful), while also providing a positive cushion to soften any downside should a crisis occur.

4 Calamities

Accidents happen – but dealing with the results needs planning

Jerry Hendin (United States),
Silvia Pendás de Cassina (Mexico)
and Jim Walsh (Ireland)

Introduction

While it is true that most crises are predictable, some happen with such speed and intensity that those affected are unable to cope with the enormity of the tragedy. In recent years we have seen natural calamities such as the tsunami in South and Southeast Asia that killed more than 200,000 people, Hurricane Katrina in Louisiana and Mississippi in the United States and earthquakes in Iran and Pakistan.

Even in business where predictability is worshipped, there are some industries – such as aviation – where, while one can predict what might happen, one cannot predict when and where it will happen. And while the world has enjoyed a remarkably solid record of safety among airlines in the past five years, when an accident does happen that results in mass fatalities, it causes untold grief for hundreds of families and grist for the media around the world.

Natural disasters and airline accidents are, for most people, one-off events. How do companies sustain their business and their reputation when they suffer multiple disasters? Those that succeed, such as those in the case studies described in this chapter, do so by reacting quickly and ensuring that they are communicating with all of their stakeholders, all of the time.

Jerry Hendin first outlines the preparation required and characteristics of a crisis in the airline industry, then Silvia Pendás de Cassina describes the reality of handling the inevitable. Finally Jim Walsh takes crisis management lessons into the realm of an accidental fire, a crisis that could affect virtually any business or organization of any size. The company described in this case study had not one but two fires – but both occurred in the space of a year.

Aeroplane accidents

Airline travel is one of the safest means of transport

Jerry Hendin

According to Geneva-based watchdog agency, the Aircraft Crashes Records Office, 2006 was one of the safest for the commercial airline industry worldwide. There were 156 crashes during the year, three-quarters of which were smaller, propeller-driven aircraft. Nearly 1,300 people lost their lives.

While 1,300 is still an unacceptably large number, it is a fraction of the nearly 2.1 billion people who flew during that period. When one compares 1,300 people to the nearly 43,000 who died in automobile accidents in just the United States in 2006, one can easily get a sense of how safe airline travel is. However, aircraft accidents, particularly those with mass fatalities, garner huge media attention around the world. This is understandable because airline accidents can change the lives of hundreds of people on a plane and tens of thousands of family members, relatives and friends.

While almost all accidents are predictable, one factor that distinguishes the airline industry from other industries is that, while one can predict what kind of on-ground or in-air accident might occur, one cannot predict where or when it will happen. This, and the number of destinations that a large company might fly to, makes flight safety a top priority for all airlines and one that is never promoted as a competitive advantage.

In general, the world's airlines do a good job of being prepared to deal with the communication issues in a crisis, but cost-cutting and other priorities have affected airlines' ability to respond in a crisis. This is particularly true when the incident or accident happens outside its home country. In the past 10 years, there have been a number of such accidents, for example Swiss

Air in Canada; Egyptair in the United States; Singapore Airlines in Taiwan; SAS in Italy; and Air China in South Korea.

A recent survey by Kenyon International Emergency Services, which has retainer contracts with more than 150 airlines around the world, found that while most airlines review, update and practise their communication plans on a regular basis at their headquarters, they are less regular about communication preparedness at outstation locations.

This is interesting because, statistically, most airline accidents happen in the first or last several minutes of flight. Also, most do not happen close to the home airport of the airline. That means that for a period of time, anywhere from the first three to 12 hours – the time when public opinion is being formed – communication is being handled by people who are less well trained than their communication counterparts at the company's headquarters.

What the world's most prepared airlines do is to continuously train their field station managers to be able to handle media enquiries, read an approved statement from headquarters or to answer questions from approved documents. In reality, during the first hours of an aeroplane accident, there is very little that one can say other than the basics of the flight – flight number, origination point and destination point – and to express to the families affected sympathy for those people who might have been injured or may have died.

In addition, the ruling aviation authority, such as the National Transportation Safety Board (NTSB) in the United States, which is responsible for investigating the accident, has very strict rules on what can and cannot be said by an airline following an accident. But by allowing field personnel, such as station managers, to address the media in the first few hours, it helps to satisfy the needs of the media, in part, until a professional public relations person can be there in person.

Why don't more airlines train their outstation people to respond to the media in a crisis? Part of the answer is organizational and part financial. On the organizational front, many airlines would prefer to manage communication in a crisis from their headquarters location, and with the advances in communications and telecommunications technology this is more possible today than in the past. Having an executive on a global TV network or on a company's website with streaming video, however, is very different to having the same executive at or near the accident site where families may have congregated and the media certainly will have gathered. It also denies the reality of today's 24/7 media environment and the desire on the part of the media to 'get' what is a dramatic, and at the same time, very tragic human interest story.

The other reality is that there will be media at the site of an incident or accident and they will expect to get information from or about the company. There will also be media at the originating destination and at the final destination, no matter where the accident may have occurred. If the company is unable to provide information, the media will get it from other sources who might have been affected by the accident; might have witnessed it; or who might have special, and not always unbiased, interest in the accident.

In addition, if an accident happens in a country with a different language or markedly different culture, the best headquarters' communication expert will quickly find him or herself out of their depth. And how the media covers an accident is directly proportional to the impact of the accident in that market in terms of its citizens injured or lost.

On the financial front, the fact is that regular training does cost money and the world's airlines have lost billions of dollars in this century. Traditional or legacy carriers have seen increased competition from low-cost carriers and all airlines have been hit by skyrocketing fuel costs.

Some airlines have found alternative ways of protecting their reputation during an accident by using a code-share or airline alliance partner communication team, hiring a 'local' public relations agency on a limited basis or using their emergency response management partner's communication resources. These alternatives are not always ideal as they delegate the reputation of the company to another source, but they have proven surprisingly effective in supporting the airline's communication resources. Star Alliance is an example of this: it has a crisis manual in place and assigns member airlines to assist in accidents in specific parts of the world.

A former senior airline industry executive used to argue that when you say your company is 'different', you stop learning from other companies. If this is so, what can other companies learn from the experience of airlines?

Despite the best planning, incidents and accident do happen and they don't always happen at a convenient time or in a con-

venient place. And for companies that operate in multiple locations in a country or around the world, they need to have a crisis
communication plan in every facility and, in a crisis that involves
fatalities, they need the ability to respond to the media with some
basic information as soon as possible. No matter the crisis, how
a company responds, or is seen to respond in a crisis, is often
more important to the public than the crisis itself.

Natural disasters

I was extraordinarily privileged to help represent my client, the
world's largest disaster management company, during two of the
largest natural disasters in this century, the tsunami in South and
Southeast Asia in December 2004 and Hurricane Katrina in Louisiana
and Mississippi in August 2006.

While hundreds of lessons were learnt by the companies and individuals who gave assistance during these two disasters, some of them
also apply to public relations professionals who might be called upon
to help. For me, the three top lessons learnt, and relearnt, were:

1. *Take care of yourself.* This seems simple enough, but under crisis
   conditions you may find yourself without enough sleep, without
   proper nutrition and without your normal support system. And
   this condition may last for days or weeks so you have to find ways
   to replenish your system by finding a place to take a 'power' nap or
   eat a 'power' bar. You also need to let your family or your support
   group (who may be thousands of miles away) know where you are
   and how you are so they can feel more comfortable in your
   absence and so that they can lend whatever support they can from
   afar.
2. *Be prepared.* That means you need to have the tools of your trade
   such as cellular phones, computers, as well as power cords and
   power adapters if in a different country. You need to make sure
   your passport is up to date and that you have proper entry visas to
   other countries. You need to have the proper clothing as well as
   vaccinations for the location you are going to. And you will need
   any medication that you take on a regular basis that may be
   unavailable in the place that you are going. You will also need
   money, and money in the right denominations, in those cases
   where a credit card may not work.

3. *Expect the unexpected.* During the tsunami, my client had to build holding structures in Thailand, but had insufficient funds to pay local contractors to do the work and the ATMs in the region would dispense only very small amounts. In New Orleans, there was insufficient room available for the thousands of workers who came to assist in reconstruction efforts, the telephones worked intermittently and travel within the city was both difficult and treacherous. Utilities were inconsistent and food was hard to find. A trip that under normal conditions might be 30 minutes could turn into one of 150 minutes, and those people who were expecting you on time in one location had probably moved to the next location to meet someone else.

Being prepared: Alaska Airlines 261

Silvia Pendás de Cassina

> Nobody wants to lose a loved one, a daughter or a son. Nobody thinks that it will happen to their family.
> Father of Alaska Airlines 261 victim

Introduction

Being prepared for a crisis made all the difference when, in this case, an air accident occurred. Being prepared means having a plan to hand ready to implement when there is a crisis. This allows one to concentrate and focus on what needs to be done and act quickly, rather than start figuring out what actions to take. Time is of the essence in a crisis, especially when we are talking about an aeroplane accident that involves the loss of many lives. By acting quickly and diligently, the company will be perceived as honest, caring and facing up to the facts no matter how grave the situation. We have selected this case study of an Alaska Airlines jetliner that went down off the coast of California in 2000. We hope this experience will be of value when the inevitable occurs without notice.

The company

Alaska Airlines is the ninth largest US airline based on passenger traffic and is the dominant US West Coast air carrier. Headquartered in Seattle, WA, Alaska Airlines carries more passengers between the state of Alaska and the Lower 48 than any other airline. During recent years, the airline has expanded significantly to serve more US East Coast, Mexican and Canadian destinations.

Long known for its Alaskan roots, symbolized by the Inuit painted on the tail of the aircraft, Alaska Airlines offers a friendly and relaxed style of service, one that passengers have come to appreciate as the 'Alaska Spirit'. The airline is also known for embracing innovative technology to improve the customer experience.

Alaska celebrated its 75th anniversary in 2007. The carrier traces its roots back to 1932, when Linious 'Mac' McGee of McGee Airways started flying his three-seater Stinson between Anchorage and Bristol Bay, Alaska. A merger with Star Air Service in 1934 created the largest airline in Alaska, which eventually became Alaska Airlines. Alaska and its sister carrier, Horizon Air, are owned by Alaska Air Group.

The challenge

On 31 January 2000, about 16:21 Pacific standard time, Alaska Airlines Inc, flight 261, a McDonnell Douglas MD-83, N963AS, went down in the Pacific Ocean about 2.7 miles north of Anacapa Island, California, close to Los Angeles. The two pilots, three cabin crew, and 83 passengers on board were killed, and the aeroplane was destroyed on impact. Flight 261 was operating as a scheduled international passenger flight under the provisions of Code 14 of Federal Regulations Part 121 from Lic Gustavo Diaz Ordaz International Airport, Puerto Vallarta, Mexico, to Seattle-Tacoma International Airport, with an intermediate stop planned at San Francisco International Airport. Visual meteorological conditions prevailed for the flight, which operated on an instrument flight rules flight plan. It was a beautiful sunny afternoon.

When Silvia Pendás SA first found out about the accident, we immediately contacted our client, Boeing Commercial Airplanes, to discuss an action plan for putting out a statement in Spanish, since the flight had originated in Mexico. A few minutes later we received a call from our client asking if we could support Alaska in its communication needs in Mexico during this terrible crisis. The Alaska Airlines PR team wanted to make sure the communication efforts they were implementing in the US would also be carried out in Mexico. Mexico was becoming an important market for them and they were planning further expansion into the region. They were concerned about the damage the accident would cause the airline locally.

At that time the airline had been flying mostly to beach destinations in Mexico. In this case, the Mexicans who died were from Puerto Vallarta. But most of the passengers were US citizens, including a number of Alaska and Horizon employees and family members.

We told Alaska's PR team in Seattle that all communications needed to be translated into Spanish. It is not culturally correct to distribute information to media in a foreign language: your client will be perceived as insensitive to the culture. Since time was of utmost importance in this case, we began distributing information immediately. As news became available, we continued to put out almost hourly statements to the local and national media.

When a crisis of this magnitude occurs, initially there is usually very little information on what happened. Sometimes months go by before the authorities determine the cause of the accident. It is important to note that when there is a plane accident, the investigation is taken over by the authorities, in this case the National Transportation Safety Board (NTSB). The airline is there to help, as well as the aeroplane manufacturer, but the NTSB heads the investigation. Nevertheless, you have to issue an initial statement with the facts as quickly as possible so that the media perceive the company as being open in its line of communication. There were several days of intense work, answering media queries, keeping a log of all telephone calls and conversations with the media, coordinating with Seattle, etc. The PR team in Seattle prepared a Q&A for the Alaska Airlines spokesperson in Mexico and for media queries. We were aware that the timing in everything we did was crucial to Alaska's image in this market, as well as the transparency of the communication. We wanted to avoid any type of speculation coming from the media. Lack of information is the best way to start speculation.

Even though all media briefings/press conferences were being conducted in the United States, we briefed Alaska Airlines' general manager in Mexico on talking to the media at a time of crisis. We were sure he would be approached by journalists in Puerto Vallarta, where he had gone to assist the family members of the passengers. The basics we gave him were:

1. Prepare for the interview. Think of what you are going to say.
2. Express condolences. There has been tremendous loss of lives not only of passengers, but of fellow workers and their families. The airline is also in mourning.

3. Do not speak off the record/do not speculate. Only speak of what you know and what is confirmed (facts).
4. Know your facts and concentrate on your messages. In this case some of the messages were: 'This is a terrible tragedy, our thoughts and prayers go out to the victims and their families. We have also lost colleagues and friends on this flight; it is a time of mourning. We are here in Puerto Vallarta to assist and attend to the needs of the family members. The airline is working closely with the authorities to determine the cause of this accident.'
5. Do not talk or answer questions about actions that are the responsibility of the investigating authorities. You say you cannot answer that question since it is for the authorities to answer.
6. Answer all other questions. If you cannot answer a question, say you will check and get back to the reporter.
7. Be honest. You are representing the company; you do not want to be perceived as trying to withhold information.

Some of the information initially distributed was:

- Initial statement with facts on the aeroplane, flight number, number of passengers and crew members, route, etc, including condolences.
- Alaska Airlines company information.
- Alaska Airlines safety record.
- MD-80 safety record.
- As information became available, press releases on the following topics were issued: list of passengers, names of crew members, formation of a team of volunteers called 'CARE' to assist with the grief of victims' families and the creation of a foundation to help raise money for them.

The results

A company can spend years building an image and a reputation and can lose it in seconds in such a crisis. The airline industry is safer than ever and aeroplane manufacturers and airlines set safety as their priority, but accidents do occur and can happen anywhere. It is a great tragedy for an airline and the most important element in all of this is to be prepared. A company must have a communication plan in place in case of an accident, which it can implement the moment it occurs.

In the case of Alaska Airlines, it had such a plan and everyone involved knew their responsibilities and roles and acted quickly. Time is essential in a situation like this. The airline lived up to the moment, faced the situation and did what it was supposed to do.

We in Mexico had excellent support from the Alaska Airlines PR team; without their support we would not have been able to do our work and react quickly to the challenges ahead. There were no gaps in the information and the media were thankful for the information passed to them in a timely manner.

Of course the news of the accident dominated the media for days, but the important fact here was that no speculative or sensationalist articles were published. The media reported on what was distributed to them, and Alaska's General Manager in Mexico did a great job in the interviews, which also aired on national television. As news of the investigation developed, the media continued to report on it.

Local dailies reported that relatives of Gabriela Chavez, a Mexican woman who died in the accident, had requested that her body be recovered and flown back to Puerto Vallarta. The media also announced that the MD-83's two flight recorders were found, 200 metres underwater off the California coastline. Mexican media stressed the consistent support and guidance provided to the families and friends of the victims by Alaska's CARE team. According to *Mexico Hoy*, aircraft in the MD-80/90 range are considered safe and efficient by the commercial aviation industry in general, despite the tragic fate of Alaska Airlines' MD-83. That same article went on to state that the accident came as a complete surprise, given that the airline had had an impeccable safety record since it began operating in Mexico years earlier.

Likewise, *El Sol de México* business and financial columnist Edgar Gonzalez acknowledged Alaska Airlines' quick response and praised its efforts to keep the Mexican media fully informed of events relating to the accident (see Figure 4.1).

Translation: *El Sol de México*, 3 February 2000, Los Capitales:

Alaska Airlines. In the midst of all the pain caused by the Alaska Airlines accident, it is important to acknowledge that the airline maintained an excellent level of communication with both the print and electronic media. The situation was handled in such a professional manner, on this occasion very correctly, that it should serve as an example to other airlines which find themselves in similar situations and which limit their efforts to sticking their heads into the ground like ostriches. Once again, another congratulations note for the Silvia Pendás PR agency. (Edgar González)

The final report from the National Transportation Safety Board determined that the probable cause of this accident was a loss of aeroplane pitch control resulting from the in-flight failure of the horizontal stabilizer trim system jackscrew assembly's acme nut threads. The NTSB conclusions were forwarded to the Federal Aviation Administration (FAA), which in turn issued the appropriate directives to be carried out on all MD-80/90s.

* Daimler-Chrysler, Alaska Airlines

****

En medio de todo el dolor por el fatal accidente del avión de Alaska Airlines, es importante destacar que la aerolínea mantuvo un excelente nivel de comunicación a través de los medios tanto impresos como electrónicos. Esta forma profesional de tratar un asunto, en esta ocasión ciertamente penoso debería de servir de ejemplo a otras aerolíneas que en casos similares se limitan, como las avestruces a esconder la cabeza. Otra felicitación para la agencia de relaciones públicas Silvia Pendás.

****

Figure 4.1 *El Sol de México*, 3 February 2000

Conclusion

From a communication standpoint, the final result was very little damage to Alaska Airlines' image in Mexico. The media took this accident as an example of how to handle a crisis and how Alaska Airlines helped them by providing information to them in Spanish in a timely and proper manner. Again, being prepared made all the difference. They also appreciated the fact that Alaska had someone locally they could talk to. Today Alaska has expanded its routes in Mexico with successful operations in the region.

When fire strikes – twice

Jim Walsh

Many companies and organizations manage to exist without suffering from a crisis that disrupts their business. Many others suffer one crisis in their lifetime. Rarely do organizations feel the effects of two similar crises in a short space of time.

Johnson & Johnson and Tylenol come to mind. The two crises that struck Johnson & Johnson within a few years of each other have been well documented. They are held up as an excellent example of how to manage a crisis and how to not just protect, but enhance, the organization's reputation.

Irish supermarket chain Superquinn also faced two similar crises within two years in the mid-1980s and although the business was severely disrupted on both occasions the company's reputation did not suffer. In fact the business – which was family-owned at the time – went on to expand and last year the Quinn family sold the business for €450 million. The way Superquinn handled both crises is an excellent example of how proper communication and a desire to place the welfare of customers and staff in the forefront of its action programme paid dividends.

The first crisis struck in September 1985. On a Sunday evening fire broke out in the Superquinn store in Blanchardstown, a new and growing suburb of the capital city, Dublin. Blanchardstown was targeted as one of the new satellite towns being built on the outskirts of the city. It was therefore a centre of fierce competition for the grocery retail trade.

Apart from Superquinn there was also a Quinnsworth Store (now Tesco) close by and a Dunnes Store in the area. Quinnsworth and Dunnes were the clear market leaders in the retail grocery sectors. Between them they had almost half of the national trade in the sector. Superquinn on the other hand had only a handful of stores concentrated in the Dublin area. In order to compete with its larger rivals it had set out its stall as a provider of quality fresh food and a reputation for innovative customer service.

It was the first grocery chain in Ireland to establish customer focus groups, the first to provide in-house offerings in fresh meat and bakery, the first to provide child-minding playrooms, the first to provide umbrellas for customers when it rained and the first to remove confectionery from beside checkouts in response to requests from parents. To ensure its customers received the best attention in its stores, Superquinn employed more people per premises than any of its rivals. The business benefit was that it was able to sell fresh goods at a premium price.

Its charismatic owner, Feargal Quinn, had established an international reputation in the industry and, as a result, he introduced many innovations in customer service from around the world. He went on to become a respected Senator in the Irish Parliament and wrote a best-selling book, *Crowning the Customer*. The innovation and positive reputation that Superquinn had acquired was to be crucial when fire struck, not once but twice.

Within 12 hours of the fire in its Blanchardstown store – it happened in the middle of the night and as a result there was no loss of life – the board of Superquinn had moved to implement a range of actions. The first decision was to demolish what remained of the store and rebuild from the ground up. Two factors influenced that decision. One was the need to preserve its reputation for freshness. While it could have continued to trade in the part of the store that was not damaged by the fire, it believed that its reputation for freshness would be difficult to sustain in that environment. The second factor was that it had been considering a revamp of the store and had drawn up plans for this.

Superquinn decided on a number of actions to preserve as many jobs as possible while the rebuilding was underway. It also had a communication programme to keep the local community informed of progress. Both of these actions became inextricably linked and helped retain a high level of customer loyalty.

Many Superquinn employees were transferred to its other stores in the Dublin area and others continued to work on the Blanchardstown site in what was a stroke of genius in retaining business. A temporary office was erected in the car park of the demolished premises and a fleet of small coaches hired. Customers were offered the opportunity to travel by coach to the nearest Superquinn store to Blanchardstown, which was in Finglas, about three miles away. For those whose grocery order would be too large to carry to and from the coaches, Superquinn had staff on site who would take the customer's order, travel to Finglas and return with the necessary order. This had the benefit of offering customers a viable alternative to transferring their custom to Quinnsworth or Dunnes and secured employment for a number of the Blanchardstown staff. The range of activities also provided fuel for an intensive communication campaign over the 10 weeks it took to rebuild the store, an extraordinary achievement in itself.

On the Monday afternoon following the fire, Superquinn's marketing manager had assembled its public relations, advertising and promotional service providers and instructed them to draw up a communication programme within 24 hours. The objective was to keep the 20,000 homes in the area of the store fully informed of the measures being made to replace it as quickly as possible and the customer service programme in place to offer them an alternative shopping experience.

The public relations company was challenged to produce a newsletter every three weeks while the rebuilding work was in progress. The first edition carried photographs of the exterior and interior of the damaged building and messages of congratulations to the fire service personnel and emergency services that had responded so quickly, and to the many businesses and individuals who had offered to help in returning the company to being a successful business. It also described what was being done to accommodate customers and staff.

The second edition three weeks later carried photographs of the progress being made on the new building and interviews with customers who had the opportunity of having their shopping collected from another store for them. Interestingly, it reminded many of the era when groceries could be ordered and delivered.

The final newsletter showed the almost finished building, a sketch of the new internal layout, and carried messages from the manager and heads of departments. It also announced the date on which the new store would open.

While the newsletter programme was in progress, an advertising campaign using local press and roadside posters was also introduced. This had a D-Day theme with the advertisement reminding consumers just how quickly progress was being made and that the re-opening was getting closer.

Superquinn had never opened a new store with fanfare. Its philosophy was that a major event with, for example, a celebrity cutting the tape or other promotional activities, would result in large crowds and those present would not fully appreciate the environment that had been created to make shopping a pleasurable experience. The re-opening of Blanchardstown was no different. However, there was a pre-opening function to acknowledge all those who had been instrumental in bringing the store back to life. These included the fire service personnel and police who had responded on the night of the fire, and their families. This gesture was extremely well received and generated considerable goodwill and publicity.

Within a short time of the store re-opening it was trading at the levels prior to the fire. This was primarily as a result of the quick and decisive decisions made immediately after the fire and the reputation for excellent customer service built-up in the 10 years it had been open prior to the fire. Superquinn Blanchardstown is still operating very successfully 20 years later, and it has been reported that its new owners are planning a revamp, with no fire to prompt them.

Fire strikes again

On 26 September 1986, almost exactly one year following the fire at its Blanchardstown store, Superquinn again had to face the consequences of an accidental fire. This time it was on the other side of Dublin, in Sutton. On this occasion the consequences were even more serious, as Sutton was not only a flagship store but the complex also incorporated the company's head office. It was known as the Support Office, which conveyed to everyone there that their primary role was to support the retail branches, which were its customers' focus.

The circumstances this time were very different to the ones in Blanchardstown. Superquinn was the only supermarket chain based in this area. The fire was more severe and there was no question but that the entire complex had to be replaced. This could clearly not be completed in 10 weeks. With both the Support Office and the shop area needing rebuilding, there were opportunities to restructure the layout and to expand the store's footprint. This required new plans and, more crucially, it needed planning permission from the local authority. The planning process in Ireland is staged and allows for local residents to have an input and, more important, object to most new building developments, if they desire.

By 1986 Superquinn had been in existence for more than 20 years and had built up a property portfolio outside of its retail premises. The company's policy had been to buy, not rent, its premises and in many cases it also owned the centres in which its stores were positioned. One of these centres was in

Blackrock, directly across Dublin Bay from Sutton. It moved all of its Support Office functions to Blackrock while the planning process and construction work in Sutton progressed.

It was to be over a year before the Sutton shop re-opened and longer before the Support Office functions moved back. During that time there was a communication programme in operation but it was not as intense as in Blanchardstown.

If it is true that no two crises are the same or can be managed in exactly the same way, Superquinn is no exception. The differences were not just in the timescale or the extent of the fires. The inclusion of the Support Office that contained all of the systems and records for the business brought a different dimension.

This was dramatically outlined by the then Chairman of Superquinn, Vincent O'Doherty, speaking at a conference on crisis management organized in 1990 in Dublin by Walsh Public Relations and the *Sunday Business Post*. He described the lessons they had learnt from the Blanchardstown fire and, significantly, the need to protect business records and to have adequate insurance cover:

> Our insurance was 100 per cent, our valuations were up-to-date, we were thoroughly covered for everything that might occur. We were excellently served by both our broker and insurance company. I had the insurance broker on the site at 8 o'clock the morning following the fire and he was able to assure me that we were fully covered.
>
> I had in my hands the afternoon of that day a seven-figure cheque and I don't think that you can do better in the way of insurance than that. That was a vital reassurance and allowed us to move on and make decisions as quickly as possible.
>
> One aspect of the insurance which turned out to be most critical for us was the so-called consequential loss cover for the effects on your bottom line of loss of business, not only when you are totally out of business but during the period in which you recover and are attempting to restore your business.
>
> The reasons why companies go out of business in occurrence of a fire, very largely has to do with the destruction of their records. We were very heavily computerized and every bit of financial and management accounting is on computer. We followed the discipline that every computer company will tell you to observe, which is that you should duplicate your records and take them out of the building.

We had a routine that every Friday evening a briefcase left the building with up-dated tapes of all our records, files, stocks, price files, management and financial accounts, the lot. On the morning the fire occurred, it was possible for the accountant to go down the road to a neighbouring house, which was owned by one of our senior executives, and collect the financial records of the company in a brief case. We took them into Digital's office on the North Circular Road and we had the company's records on computer that same day. We paid the wages that Friday by re-running the run of the previous week and we paid the creditors that Thursday.

Unusually, the two crises that Superquinn faced resulted in very little media involvement. While Superquinn and its owner were well known throughout the country through its innovations and the PR-savvy nature of the business, these crises were local. Apart from reporting on the fires and the occasional media enquiry about rebuilding progress, there was little media interest. The focus in each case was on direct business-to-customer communication and to emphasize the company's reputation as an organization that cares about its customers and staff.

The lesson for board and senior managers faced with similar situations is: act fast. Clear and decisive decision making is crucial, as is preparation to ensure business continuity and well directed communication. And, crucially, don't desert your principles. Don't change your behaviour. The decision to rebuild rather than repair Superquinn in Blanchardstown was driven by the need to preserve a reputation for freshness.

If a business has a clear focus and has a reputation built on clear principles, deserting these principles in time of crisis will make it difficult, if not impossible, to recover from any damage caused by the crisis.

Conclusion

This chapter has dealt with what could be described as accidents waiting to happen – in the sense that airline crashes are as predicable as crashes in any form of transport and that fire can strike anywhere at any time to any building.

It is one thing to anticipate a likely event; however it is another to be prepared when the accident happens. All airlines must have plans for dealing with the aftermath of an air crash and even if they do not have a contingency for any other eventuality, all businesses should have a plan in the event of a fire at their place of business. The lesson from this chapter is: be prepared.

Most organizations have a business contingency plan but not all pay sufficient attention to being prepared to communicate, not just through the media but directly with a range of stakeholders. When an accident happens, whether it is an airline crashing, a fire, an explosion, a tsunami or a hurricane, being prepared allows senior management to make decisions quickly and authoritatively.

A crisis can be defined as an event that has one or more of the following characteristics: it disrupts normal business; it has the potential to close a business permanently; it requires an immediate coordinated management response; and it focuses media attention on an organization. Serious accidents as described here have all these characteristics.

5 The new dynamics of financial crisis

How public companies should prepare for the worst

Tim Wallace (United States)

Introduction

Several years ago, Nike Corporation faced a consumer boycott over charges that management were employing underage and underpaid Asian shoe workers. As street theatre, the protest was hugely successful. Media from around the world reported on young people, many of them inner city youths, returning their Nikes in huge piles in front of retail locations in major cities globally. But as an economic weapon the effect was negligible. Nike demonstrated to its analysts and institutional investors that the boycott was having little material impact on retail sales, and that the company's projected financial outlook remained largely unaffected.

It wasn't long, nonetheless, before Nike faced a financial crisis. As the protest gathered steam, Nike stock began to lose momentum. At its nadir, the stock had plunged by one-third, representing billions of dollars in lost value. It didn't seem to matter to investors that the company's income statement was holding up. Before long, Nike was at the negotiating table and its financial plight was widely seen as a major reason why.

This story suggests some of the new dynamics of financial crisis. For public companies (which are the focus of this chapter), crises that initially have little to do with the income statement have a tendency to quickly assume financial implications. In fact, in a world of global markets and instant communication, it might be said that for public companies nearly every serious crisis today is an incipient financial crisis.

But there is more. Financial crises have a damaging ripple effect. They can open a second front in the original crisis or spark a new one in its own right. In a culture where financial news has entered the mainstream, notably through the impact of the internet and blogs, reports of a company's weakening stock price can convince the public that the marketplace has spoken and that the disease must be as serious as its critics charge. Finally, important changes among institutional investors, perhaps the most important financial constituents for a public company, have made such investors agents of restructuring and, in this sense, abettors of crisis.

In short, today's financial crises are especially insidious and ubiquitous, in many ways unique among the categories of crisis treated in this book. It is essential that management first appreciate the new dynamics of financial crisis – specifically how they are part and parcel of all types of crisis and what, in a global marketplace, the forces are that encourage them. Next, they need to assess whether the organization is prepared – by way of organizational structure and spokesperson preparation – to successfully navigate the critical opening phases of any financial crisis. Finally, they must focus on preventive measures that can be taken now, at a time when financial communication is perhaps more complicated than ever, to strengthen the organization's reputation with key financial audiences. These are the themes that we will address in this chapter.

Understanding financial crisis

The new dynamics

If we were asked to define financial crisis, most of us would probably point to the accounting scandals that drove companies such as Enron, WorldCom and Tyco out of existence. Here the dots connected quite nicely: the company did something egregious financially and it suffered commensurate financial consequences.

But it should be plain that, as Nike's 'unsuccessful' boycott demonstrates, financial crises are not always so clear-cut. Many financial crises are stock-driven and, as the boxed text below demonstrates, declining stock price, when it attains sufficient velocity, depth and duration, represents a crisis in and of itself.

We may understand instinctively that jittery investors sell on bad news of any kind. But it is not always clear why exactly this happens –

why the image of a pile of trainers can spark widespread selling in a hard-nosed, ROI-focused global investment marketplace when the P&L impact seems marginal. The answer has to do with the interaction of public equity and corporate reputation.

Many of us instinctively view stock performance as the quintessential financial measure, one that reflects almost exclusively either actual or anticipated value on the income statement. Clearly, a major component of any company's valuation lies in financial fundamentals. But a large and growing body of research has demonstrated the influence of non-financial measures on market valuation. Ernst & Young's classic 'Measures That Matter' study attributes 35 per cent of a company's value to non-financial intangibles. The American Institute of Certified Public Accountants (AICPA) recently stated that 'a number of intangible drivers can give business leaders a better perspective on where value is created, over and above what they would get looking at standard financial reporting metrics'.

Essentially, these 'intangible drivers' include the qualities that communication executives ascribe to corporate reputation – things such as the power of the brand, customer satisfaction, clarity of strategic direction, service quality and perceptions of management strength and integrity. If you have trouble seeing how these kinds of intangibles represent value, imagine if some sort of disaster destroyed all of Coca-Cola's physical assets, its bottling plants, distribution network and its workforce. Bankers would stand in line to lend the company money, with only one thing serving as collateral: reputation.

Given this, it is hardly surprising that stock acts as a proxy for corporate reputation. When a crisis negatively impacts reputation – be it a calamity, fraud, product tampering or a highly visible consumer boycott – reputation value is destroyed, and this resonates in the stock price.

The perils of declining stock price

We know instinctively that a declining stock price is undesirable. But it is worth reviewing why a serious and steadily eroding stock price – whatever the cause – constitutes a crisis in its own right for a public company:

- A declining valuation potentially constricts growth because it increases a company's cost of capital, which in turn makes many strategic business options either more expensive or even prohibitive.
- Loss of valuation opens a second front in the communication battle, awakening concerns from a fresh group of powerful constituents – investment analysts, institutional investors, the financial media, individual shareholders and others.

- Sell-side analysts are critical third parties in building and sustaining a company's brand reputation. They are also as skittish as mares and as memory-retentive as elephants. When a company makes them look bad with a downside surprise, it may take a long time to win back their full trust.
- Declining stock may harm the morale of key executive employees, whose compensation is often linked to some degree to the performance of company equity.
- Finally, as illustrated in Figure 5.1, when a crisis drives down stock it sets up a negative feedback loop in which the decline is taken as evidence of corporate weakness or even guilt, which in turn further depresses the stock, and so on.

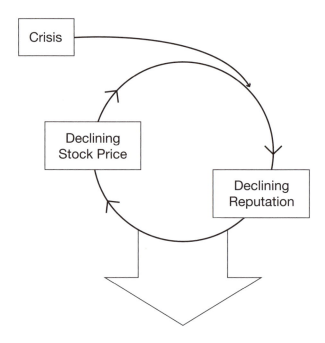

Figure 5.1 The final crisis feedback loop

Stock price and corporate reputation are inextricably linked. For public companies, most crises that impact corporate reputation quickly reverberate in the stock price, which in turn further harms corporate reputation.

Institutional investors: potential agents of crisis

The other important new dynamic of financial crisis relates to changes in a critical audience segment for the public company: the institutional shareholder.

The institutional universe has exploded in terms of size in the past 20 years. The number of institutions investing in equities has more than tripled since the late 1980s. Growth in funds under management has been even more dramatic, expanding more than 15-fold in that time. Hedge funds, the more shadowy part of the institutional market, have grown even more dramatically: by some estimates there are about 8,000 hedge funds today with combined assets of about US $1 trillion, up from US $400 billion in 2001. Because hedge funds can leverage, their impact on the markets is probably far larger.

Not only has the institutional market grown, but also its behaviour has changed in ways that have important crisis implications. Experts talk about the evolution of pension funds from owners to agents. While we are now seeing something of a counter-trend, pension funds have largely outsourced day-to-day portfolio management to third-party asset managers. Pension funds increasingly act like a fund of funds manager regarding the actively managed portion of their portfolio, overseeing advisers rather than assets.[1] The market has become even more intensely returns-driven, where poor performing asset managers can be easily replaced, where sophisticated performance monitoring technology is widely employed, and where the under-funding crisis has fostered a 'beat the market' mentality at most pension funds in the United States.

How do all these trends influence the crisis calculus? First, it makes the entire institutional investment arena even more focused on the short term. As one asset manager recently put it, 'As long as client mandates (eg, pension funds) require us to deliver performance benchmarked against short-term market tracker indexes, we will of course remain short term in our outlook.' It is estimated that the average stock mutual fund today turns over its complete portfolio every year.

One might think that a quarter-to-quarter focus could make institutional shareholders less interested in the business fundamentals of their underlying investment. But in many cases precisely the opposite has occurred: institutional investors have moved from passive observers of management to, when circumstances warrant, active agents of strategic restructuring to build shareholder value.

Today's shareholder activism takes many guises, but its most powerful form has less to do with an annual meeting gadfly or a socially responsible investing advocate, than with a giant public pension fund, discretely but forcefully expressing its discontent to management and the board – often through coalitions with other major shareholders who, together, wield a very big stick. When these groups talk, boards and management listen.

The management consulting firm Booz Allen Hamilton noted in a recent study that global turnover of CEOs hit a record in 2005 (the most recent year of its research). Furthermore, four times as many of the world's top CEOs were forced out of their jobs in 2005 as in 1995. The major reason: investor discontent. 'Ten years ago,' the firm concluded, 'the CEO's job was all about "stewardship" of the corporation's assets for stakeholders; today, it's all about the bottom line for investors.'

Many hedge funds have raised shareholder activism to a new level. Here they identify underperforming companies, design what are often quick-fix solutions to boost value, accumulate a major equity stake, and then demand changes in the business strategy. If the company refuses, the dissidents often engage in a proxy fight to place their advocates on the board. According to one expert, today there are about 90 activist hedge funds worldwide compared to 40 three years ago.

We see examples of these institutionally triggered crises regularly:

- Frustrated by Home Depot's stagnant stock, institutional investors essentially forced the board to replace a highly visible and once-lauded CEO, Robert Nardelli. One newspaper cited a letter from a major institutional shareholder to the board listing long-standing 'deficiencies in strategy, operations, capital allocation and governance'.
- Citigroup recently announced its intention to lay off or reassign more than 26,000 employees worldwide as part of an effort to cut costs and streamline the bank's global operations. It was widely commented that institutional investors were the driving force behind this action.
- Billionaire financier Carl Icahn, with the backing of powerful hedge funds, managed to win himself and two allies seats on the board of Blockbuster Entertainment, the movie rental chain. Icahn's group had developed what amounted to an alternative corporate strategy for Blockbuster, encouraging acquisitions and moves to blunt the growth of online competitors.

The stock often responds well to these initiatives. But institutional activism usually has the unfortunate effect of generating a crisis for other corporate stakeholders, notably employees whose morale suffers during job cuts and local communities where the company has a diminished presence. Again, we witness the ripple effect of financial crisis.

Responding to financial crisis

Step 1: avoiding opening mistakes

Financial crises, then, have a thousand different faces. This is what makes them demanding; no two are precisely alike. But all crises share at least one thing: they compress time and force companies to act a lot faster than they would like. This is why the crisis management experts cited elsewhere in this book advocate that crisis materials – statements, press releases, fact sheets and backgrounders – be prepared in advance.

Unfortunately, many companies commit common errors in these critical opening rounds of a crisis. The most important of them stem from two basic factors: the failure of key crisis functions to mesh seamlessly (due to management and organizational flaws), and mistakes in spokesperson performance. As such, they compromise the most important goals of crisis communication: clear, credible and consistent communication.

Let's review these mistakes now.

A house divided (1): the IR/PR disconnect

Major corporations usually divide external communication duties between an investor relations (IR) and public relations (PR) department, each of which typically reports within the organization through different channels – finance and marketing, respectively. Investor and public relations are, of course, artificial divisions in the communications function, necessitated by the fact that it is hard to find the combination of strong financial and marketing skills in one individual. It is never an ideal arrangement, especially these days when IR executives often manage financial media enquiries. But in normal times, with a strict delineation of responsibilities, companies make it work.

The intensity of a crisis, however, often awakens the latent conflicts between two independent external communications functions co-existing under one roof. During a crisis, many new and unfamiliar journalists contact a company. Communication is intensified. It takes place under tight deadlines and often with adversarial undertones.

Authoritative answers are harder to come by. Journalists are largely oblivious to the PR/IR distinction (or, if they recognize it, are happy to exploit it). They will ask public relations people to clarify financial issues and investor relations people to review product or public affairs issues. In short, under crisis conditions it is easy to stray from one's competence or say things one shouldn't. The consequences, which can wind up in the morning newspapers, span the full panoply of crisis communication setbacks: inaccurate and/or inconsistent information, selective disclosure, release of confidential information and rumour.

Integration of the IR and PR functions is not something that can happen in the midst of crisis. It just doesn't work. It needs to be institutionalized long before a crisis strikes. Doing so is a function of an emerging executive position, the Chief Communication Officer (CCO). The primary task of the CCO is to manage both investor relations and public relations as an integrated communications function. He or she makes certain that IR and PR departments meet regularly, that their offices are placed in close proximity to each other, and that their compensation packages are structured to incentivize teamwork and cooperation. The CCO has ultimate responsibility for managing all corporate stakeholders, including employees, shareholders, financial analysts, public affairs and press relations.

A house divided (2): the lawyer/communications disconnect

Similar potential conflicts exist between the legal and public relations/investor relations departments. The reason has to do with a glass half full/glass half empty view of external communication. From the legal perspective, external communication usually carries down-side risk; for PR and IR executives, it's full of upside potential. When crisis strikes and communication policy becomes a strategic imperative, these views can clash.

When forced to choose between these views during a financial crisis (or for that matter, most other types of crisis), management usually adopt some variant of the legal perspective on communication. It is no mystery why. Financial communication operates within a complicated web of regulations that lawyers are often uniquely positioned to interpret. Attorneys are trained to identify risk and apprise management of what could go awry in any proposed action. Every crisis, but especially a financial crisis, involves legal risk. Many CEOs perceive both the investor relations and the public relations functions to be more technically than managerially oriented. Finally, when we are threatened, it always seems safer to be quiet and keep our head down.

The problem with an overly legal approach to crisis response is that it can encourage a hunker-down stance that cedes the high ground to critics and adversaries. Lawyers are usually conservative, and they discourage the kind of calculated risk-taking that lies behind any good communication. But successful crisis management strategies are often dramatic. It is hard to imagine, for example, that lawyers instinctively rallied around JetBlue's Customer Bill of Rights and public apology on YouTube after its crisis in the winter of 2007. Conversely, it is easy to see the hand of legal restraint in Exxon's 'no comment' stance after the *Valdez* tragedy, or in NASA's evasive and sluggish conduct after the Challenger space shuttle explosion.

The solution, again, is to assimilate both the legal and public relations perspective, and to ensure that each function is operating together as a team. Most of the time, contact between communications and legal has to do with the control and vetting of public material, and in this sense contains an element of tension. This is one reason why the kind of crisis planning and role-playing discussed elsewhere in this book, where attorneys and communications professionals practise working as a team in a simulated crisis 'wargame', are so important.

The psychology of financial crisis

Let us turn now to failures in spokesperson communication. By way of approaching the topic, it is well to pause and consider the psychological dynamics that come to the fore in the key players when a crisis first strikes.

Management and their financial audiences often have different and potentially discordant reactions in the face of a crisis. Most CEOs and top executives are can-do optimists. Unless they are facing a clear and unmitigated catastrophe, their first instinct is often to underestimate the crisis and overestimate their ability to get it fixed. Financial audiences, on the other hand, are often experiencing hyper-reality. They have been surprised, their reputations have been damaged, and they are in the dark. That place where CEO denial and the shareholder/analyst anxiety meet can be dangerous.

For the CEO spokesperson, this is not the moment for sunny-eyed optimism and sugar-coated assurances. Be determined – but above all be realistic. Remember that probably never again in the crisis will financial audiences be as prepared as they are at this moment to hear and bear the worst. Put out all the bad news that you know. Show suitable emotion. Admit what you don't know. If you think it could get worse, say so. Commit to a reasonable and workable timeframe to get answers. Begin to build back.

The initial communication

Management face two imperatives when crisis strikes. They must resolve the crisis and create the perception that they are doing so. The two can be very different. During the *Valdez* oil spill, Exxon probably did a decent job working to contain the environmental damage on Prince William Sound, but did a horrible job creating the perception that it was doing so. As a result, its name became synonymous with environmental catastrophe.

During financial crises, the perception of management competence and candour represents a bulwark against early selling of the stock, which can be self-perpetuating once it gets started. Most big investors/analysts will give management the opportunity to make their case before they decide on reducing their stake or initiating a downgrade. And even if early sell-offs weaken the stock, management can facilitate recovery (assuming they have a case to make) if they set the right tone at the outset with shareholders and analysts, and then show signs of delivering on what they promised.

Here are some of the important observations to keep in mind about communication during the first moments of a financial crisis:

● Do a conference call/webcast, and do it quickly. As alluded to earlier, the debate is usually lively about whether to risk a live audience before investors in the first 24 hours of a crisis. The question is valid because there are more uncertainties than facts in the early phases of most crises. A company must also weigh the peculiar circumstances and magnitude of a crisis, the skill level of its spokespeople, and the legal ramifications of speaking out. But as a rule of thumb, a company usually has more to lose at the outset by not communicating to investors in some real-time forum than by doing so. Put simply, investors want to hear from management in the immediate aftershock of a crisis. They want to be reassured 'eyeball-to-eyeball' that the company's leadership is prepared to resolve the problem and recover from it. These emotions, which are critical in enlisting support, cannot be replicated through prepared statements. In the absence of live communication, company statements often suggest that there is something to hide. Ideally, the CEO, CFO and other relevant corporate executives should be speaking live to financial audiences the day after a crisis breaks.

● Err on the side of caution. People tend to remember what they hear first and what they hear last. This is why, as noted earlier, unwarranted assurances and speculation in the early days of a crisis often dig spokespeople into a hole. Never say more than you know for certain. Build confidence by letting actions speak louder than words. Management do not lose credibility when they say, 'We don't know yet, but we are going to find out.' And then communicate what they find out.

- Open the door to continued communication. Financial audiences, like nature, abhor a vacuum. Shareholders and analysts want and need the assurance that they will be hearing regularly from management, whether the news is good or bad. It is essential that the company commits to providing updates as events unfold. These can take different forms – from group meetings to press releases – depending on developments.

- Be prepared. However skilled and experienced a CEO or CFO may be in investor communication, no matter how collegial a company's relationships have been with stakeholders in the past, it can be a whole different ballgame when a crisis strikes. Crisis communication is by its nature more adversarial, more probing, faster paced and less predictable. This is why all presenters should face rigorous, 'full-contact' devil's advocate questioning before any meeting. Presentations should be well rehearsed, with attention paid to cosmetic issues such as tone and pacing as well as to content.

Step 2: building reputation in 'normal time' communication

When it comes to reputation management, we don't get a second chance when crisis strikes. Much of the credibility we need during a crisis is earned before the crisis happens.

Credibility is perhaps the most precious commodity during a crisis. Investors' decisions to hold on or jump ship are influenced by reputation more than we might suspect, even in the financial arena where profit and loss issues seem determinant. The question from financial audiences, much as it is with others, becomes, 'Do I have a basis for trusting management to give me a true sense of what is going on and, ultimately, to restore value?'

That said, interaction with institutional shareholders and sell-side analysts is perhaps the most complex and demanding external relationship that public company management have to deal with. Most CEOs and CFOs are 'on stage' before these groups, via conference calls or one-to-one meetings, several times a year to review earnings and other material developments. In the era of Regulation FD, these communications now must include financial journalists. The restrictions governing financial communication are more stringent than ever, and management are usually walking a tightrope between saying too much and not saying enough. It is not hard to leave everyone dissatisfied.

In short, these interactions are ripe with opportunity but fraught with down-side risk for reputation building. Nonetheless they remain the way financial constituents form important judgements about management, centring on the types of questions that become pivotal during a crisis. They involve four basic areas:

1. *Credibility* – how have management managed corporate disappointments in the past? Did they initiate meetings to talk about it, or did they run and hide?
2. *Confidence* – have management set clear and realistic benchmarks for the business, have they delivered on what they said they would, and not hyped or over-promised?
3. *Competence* – have executive management proved that they have a grasp on the details of the business?
4. *Execution* – is there depth of management in place that can execute what needs to be done?

JetBlue has devoted considerable energy and care to these kinds of questions among its financial audiences. It had been described in some quarters as a darling of the investment community. That, of course, was before the meltdown in the winter of 2006, when the airline stranded thousands of passengers at New York's JFK Airport and kept some trapped on aircraft for up to 10 hours.

Clearly, JetBlue made critical business errors that exacerbated the crisis. Its fate was still not resolved when this book went to press. But from a financial point of view, it seems clear that the company could have fared much worse. During the month following the crisis, the stock never went below its 52-week low. And while there were investor critics, there were just as many supporters – including Merrill Lynch, which called the stock 'oversold' not long after the crisis.

In short, good communication now pays reputation dividends in crises. Here is an overview of five key programme supplements that can both improve public company communication and simultaneously help with crisis readiness:

1. Know your institutional shareholders

For this task, most companies rely on public filings, such as 13f forms in the United States. In normal times, this approach suffices for most companies. During a crisis, management need better intelligence: 13f filings only reflect an institution's position at the end of the most recent quarter, and can be filed weeks after the quarter's end. An investor who buys and sells within a quarter will never appear in a 13f filing.

Management should be familiar with various shareholder ID and surveillance services. Some of these are offered free for Nasdaq listed companies. Exchange-traded companies should maintain relations with their specialists.

2. Seek constant feedback from investor audiences

The company should survey investors that participate in quarterly earnings conference calls before and after these events. This is not only a way to keep these presentations focused and relevant, but reveals what kinds of questions investors might be asking. It also provides a precedent for gathering this kind of intelligence during crises.

3. Strengthen the IR portion of the website

The corporate website, as has been noted elsewhere in this book, is a vital crisis management tool because it can quickly distribute persuasive information to widely dispersed audiences. This potential is realized, of course, only if the company's website is up-to-date, content-rich and established as a trafficked shareholder and analyst resource before a crisis hits. Financial audiences are accustomed to working with IR portions of websites, assuming that they are robust. What constitutes a robust IR website? At a minimum, it should contain the following information:

- welcome letter/shareholder letter;
- review of the company's growth strategies;
- frequently asked questions;
- past financial presentations, including replays of webcasts;
- fact sheet;
- stock price graph;
- historical financials;
- event calendar.

4. Policy statements on key topics

The IR department should have clear, written policies, suitable for external distribution, related to trading by insiders, financial disclosure, corporate governance and other issues.

5. Periodic audit of financial audiences

Periodically, companies should conduct a formal communication audit of their shareholders and analysts. These surveys should review areas where the corporate strategy may be misunderstood, aim to reveal how communication could be improved and seek to discover new and preferred ways to reach out to these groups.

Conclusion

Financial crises have assumed new and wider dimensions that represent serious challenges for public companies. In the age of the internet and the globalization of financial markets, financial crises are rarely confined to narrow borders as in other types of crises. When a public company based in Amsterdam faces a local food tampering issue, for example, the stock valuation suffers and investors around the world sit up and take notice. Because of the internet and the growing power of blogs, declining financial performance is often circulated to and noted by non-financial audiences as well. Companies often find themselves fighting a war on two fronts. Financial markets today are also far less complacent than in the past. Institutional investors, as we have seen, face unprecedented performance pressures, and are increasingly intolerant of sustained mediocre performance. In this case, they can be active agents of change and precipitators of crises – financial and otherwise.

How does a company respond to these trends? Obviously, strong, sustained performance is the best antidote. But few companies are so fortunate, and even then no one is immune to crisis. Communication remains an important piece of the puzzle. It has to happen long before a crisis hits. If financial audiences clearly understand a company's strategic focus, and if it is presented to them in a way that is persuasive, they may show patience while the elements of that strategy fall into place. If management speak regularly with investors and analysts; if they are open to the financial media; if they habitually prepare investors for disappointment; if they treat them with candour; then each of these groups may give management a short-lived opportunity to make their case before reacting in panicked selling.

The opening moves of any crisis are always critical. This is especially true on the financial side, where shareholders are nervously watching their investment lose value. Opinions form quickly. There is no question that management can make a bad situation worse if they stumble early – send mixed messages about what is going on, or seem unre-

sponsive, unduly optimistic or evasive. These are the frequent consequences of the organizational conflicts and spokesperson pitfalls
reviewed earlier in this chapter. If management only focused on
improving their performance here, they will have taken a big step
toward minimizing the impact of financial crises and meeting what is
ultimately their most important goal: stealing a step on the road to
restoring their reputation.

Note

1. There has been recent discussion about institutions increasingly conducting their own research and portfolio management, and of the corre-
   sponding decline in sell-side research. Yet the larger trend noted here
   remains unchanged, in my view.

6 Fraud

A challenge for PR crisis management

Thom M Serafin (United States)

Introduction

Fraud is a fundamental challenge for PR crisis management and can arise in different forms. The organization you represent may be accused, fairly or unfairly, of having engaged in fraud, or your client or organization can become the victim of fraud by a rival firm or unscrupulous litigants. In either case, the reputation of the organization is at stake until the public has made a judgement on your client's actions. Accusations of fraud strike to the heart of an organization's relationship with the public, and can present obstacles that must be carefully navigated to restore credibility.

It is hard to overstate the damage to a company, governmental agency or non-profit organization when the public begins to believe it lacks basic integrity. In a relatively short span, fundamental trust, built up over many years between an organization and those it serves, can be seriously damaged. The morale within an organization and its working partners can quickly erode. The perception of fraud also carries the potential for legal problems from either regulatory agencies or law enforcement, which is yet another reason why public relations crisis management must act decisively to either demonstrate that the charge of fraud is unsubstantiated or, alternatively, that it is being effectively addressed in a transparent way that will reassure the public of the organization's reliability.

Gather the facts

As a first step, the expeditious gathering of facts is crucial, because those who speak on behalf of an organization accused of fraud need to quickly establish their own credibility to effectively rebut unsubstantiated charges. If the charge that the organization you represent made a misleading or fraudulent claim does appear to have merit, the crisis management team need to convey quickly and effectively how the problem is being (or already has been) corrected and what measures are being taken to see that it will not happen again. Conversely, if the very serious charge of fraud is unsubstantiated, a strategy to explain how and why must be developed quickly. Calls for a retraction from the party or news organization that made the charge may be appropriate.

If those in charge of crisis management find that fraud did, in fact, take place, they must quickly establish whether it was inadvertent (ie, representations made in good faith, but defeated by poor performance or unanticipated factors) or is a more serious fraud involving deliberate deceit by an individual or part of the organization. This is crucial, because in public perception the difference between unintentionally misleading communication, on the one hand, and deliberate deceit on the other, is substantial and requires very different responses on the part of the PR crisis management team.

A promise unfulfilled

An example of the former occurred when a home mortgage company that promised to process low-interest home loan applications within a specific time period was unable to keep this promise because a sudden drop in interest rates created an overload of loan applicants who wanted to refinance their homes. A Chicago-based financial columnist, who also appears regularly on local television, took up the complaints of dissatisfied applicants and began to pound the company relentlessly in both print and her television commentary.

Fact-finding by the company quickly established that the problem was widespread in the mortgage loan industry. A sudden drop in interest rates had caused a surge of applications among homeowners seeking to refinance their home mortgages. Title companies and other players in the home finance network were also overwhelmed and most mortgage companies were not able to keep up with the applications, leaving many frustrated homeowners angry at a missed opportunity to lower their monthly payments.

The fact that other companies experienced the same problem, however, did not remove the stigma of being singled out by the financial columnist, and she continued to mention complaints about the company from disgruntled applicants at every opportunity. Finally, the company decided to hire a PR firm that specialized in crisis management. As part of its press package, the team assembled a document that used government figures about home loan mortgage delays to illustrate how the problem of delayed mortgage applications was industry-wide. The company also hired more qualified staff to process loans, and promised shorter turn around time for loan applications. Most important, the company issued a Customer Bill of Rights which, among other things, guaranteed transparency and useful remedies for any problems in the application process.

The press package was distributed to financial media, both locally and nationally, which resulted in a number of print articles. At the same time, the financial columnist, who had received the press package with the Customer Bill of Rights, contacted the company and invited it to send a spokesperson to be interviewed on her television segment about how problems had been created by an overload of mortgage refinancing. In a relatively short period of time, the company went from being singled out as a laggard in performance to being viewed as an innovative problem-solver for an industry-wide problem.

Legal issues must be sorted out

Fraud can have legal implications when it is verified or admitted by the organization. Lawsuits, fines or prosecution can follow. For this reason, public relations crisis management may need to be coordinated with attorneys representing the organization. As much as possible, the PR crisis management team will need to work within guidelines established by the legal representatives of the organization accused of fraud. At the same time, there may be circumstances when legal advisers and PR management will clash over competing principles. Attorneys understandably push to limit legal exposure – that is their job. For that reason, they may advise against accepting blame or even acknowledging that a statement, guarantee or advertisement made by the client was misleading.

The public relations crisis management team, on the other hand, have a duty to explain to management the risks of denying that someone committed fraud in the organization. If someone in an organization has actually committed fraud, one should assume that the facts will eventually come to light. Management should be advised of the potential harm that may result from denying or covering up the issue of fraud, in terms of a firm's overall reputation for integrity.

Denial not only erodes precious public credibility, it delays corrective action and offers the impression that a misleading claim was not an aberration, but rather part of a pattern of deceit. Ultimately, it is management that will have to make the call on how much an organization is willing to admit. To repair damage from an accusation of fraud, the PR crisis management team must make sure that their advice is carefully weighed by management along with the advice of the legal staff.

Third-party validation

As with other aspects of effective crisis PR management, the use of respected third parties to validate facts is an important tool in the arsenal. If a company's credibility is itself under attack, then the most effective rebuttal will come from third parties, particularly government agencies or respected experts not tied to the company.

A pharmaceutical company, for instance, may have made claims about a particular prescription drug based on its own testing of the product and Federal Drug Administration (FDA) trials, yet find itself on the defensive over a new study (which may or may not be rigorous or valid). Maybe anecdotal evidence has turned up a higher incidence of serious side effects or fatalities attributed to the product.

Was the pharmaceutical company guilty of fraud when it attested to the safety of the product? The answer is no, but to effectively rebut the claim, it needs to act promptly, not only in providing helpful data from FDA testing, but also providing supportive articles from prominent medical journals or by mobilizing respected physicians to speak on the company's behalf.

Respected third parties can also vouch for your client's history over the long run. If your client has developed a good reputation gained over many years, third parties can remind them of this fact, which would put any charge of fraud in perspective. If the public is convinced that a claim was made in good faith by a company recognized as a good corporate citizen, the damage from a claim that turned out be mistaken will be seen in perspective.

Delay and denial compound the problem

Despite high profile scandals such as the Enron debacle, there is little evidence that out-and-out premeditated fraud is a widespread problem in western corporate culture today. What helped doom the high-flying Enron management was the perception of extreme arrogance, as exemplified when Enron CEO Jeff Skilling – now serving a long prison term but then at the height of his power – ridiculed a reporter on a conference call. He called the reporter an 'asshole' when the reporter had the temerity to ask about misleading statements in Enron's financial reporting.

Interestingly, a recent article on Enron notes that many of the questionable financial schemes used by the company were actually outlined in its reports and argues that investors who performed due diligence were not misled by the company's management. Arrogance, however, was rampant in Enron's corporate culture and this tendency can blind some organizations to what the press and the public will conclude when unpleasant facts come to light. If Enron had acknowledged accounting and reporting mistakes early on, if it had taken corrective action when the first inquiries were being made by *Fortune Magazine* and a few other publications, would the company have collapsed so quickly and irreversibly? Perhaps not.

A powerful corporation may even be successful in keeping news organizations from reporting allegations or evidence of fraud, but that strategy is seldom effective in the long run, and it keeps the controversy alive.

Denial and delay

When ABC News reported in 1994 that Brown and Williamson, a major tobacco company, covered up research data suggesting that the company 'spiked' nicotine levels to keep cigarette users hooked on the habit, the company sued for libel the researcher who had provided corporate documents to the network. The company also sued ABC for a record US $10 billion. Other news organizations, including the *New York Times* and CBS *Sixty Minutes* were threatened with similar lawsuits and both initially withheld reports that had been prepared by investigative reporters.

Brown and Williamson's bold but misguided effort to intimidate news organizations proved to be a public relations nightmare, because the evidence of manipulation of nicotine levels had emerged from its own research department and other news organizations continued to report these findings. A critically acclaimed Hollywood film, *The Insider* detailed the effort by the tobacco company to cover up the findings of its own researcher and the harassment he experienced. It was against this background of denial and obfuscation that some of the large settlements were won on behalf of individuals who had suffered from lung disease attributed to smoking.

By disputing unpleasant facts instead of acknowledging them and taking corrective action, a client faces a much longer and more difficult path to restoring its credibility with the media. By delaying the inevitable reckoning, the public perception of integrity that enables your client to function effectively in the public sphere will be seriously compromised.

When your client is a victim of fraud

When your client is on the receiving end of fraudulent accusations, PR crisis management faces a similar challenge to gather facts quickly and communicate them effectively to all the parties the organization serves. The crisis management team must consider the consequences of short- and long-term strategies to make it clear that the client was the victim of a fraud and that information is or will soon be available to support this statement.

Fingered

A classic case of this type was the fraudulent claim by a customer of Wendy's Hamburgers outlet in San Jose, California, to have found part of a finger in her bowl of chilli. It would certainly have been a disquieting finding, had it actually happened, but the company suspected that the partial finger had actually been placed there by the accuser. Unable to prove that immediately, the dilemma faced by the company was described by the company's CEO:

> In the early hours of this crisis, we were faced by demanding questions and choices. The Wendy's brand and our reputation as a quality restaurant were at stake. And just as importantly the livelihood of our employees was at risk.

Because of the grim 'discovery', Wendy's soon became fodder for jokes on Jay Leno's *Tonight* show. The San Jose outlet saw its business fall by 50 per cent. The customer made it clear she was considering a lawsuit.

The company took the first step of crisis management by gathering the relevant facts. Without the facts to back it up, the company would have experienced a major negative reaction had it voiced its suspicion that a customer had placed part of a finger in the chilli bowl. The company gave its employees lie-detector tests and checked suppliers' safety records to assure itself that the finger segment had not been served in the chilli bowl.

Within 24 hours, the company was confident that it had been the victims of a ruse. Yet it still faced a public relations dilemma and decision. It could settle quietly with the customer and perhaps slow the torrent of negative press and jokes on late night television, or hope that law enforcement would successfully reveal the fraud and blackmail.

Schuessler writes, 'It might have been expedient to pay off the accuser in an attempt to end the media onslaught – after all that is the preferred capitulation in the trial lawyer-driven age.' The company says it never considered doing so and sought to work with the police to uncover the fraud.

The offer of a reward of $100,000 for information on the investigation was a wise PR crisis management move. In doing so, the company shifted the focus to finding information that would exonerate it and implicate the accuser. The reward also demonstrated the company's confidence that it was in the right from the beginning and its belief that it would be cleared of responsibility for the grotesque 'discovery'.

The short-term problem might have been finessed by paying off the accuser, but the longer-term implications for a firm such as Wendy's that had cultivated an image as a family friendly franchise, carefully nurtured by its affable founder Dave Thomas, meant that such a strategy would have left a cloud over its reputation.

Just because an organization finds itself the innocent victim of fraud it does not mean that it should not adopt the techniques of crisis PR management. On the contrary, the public needs to be reminded that the organization is doing everything it can to prevent such incidents.

The Tylenol case (see Chapter 1), is another extreme example of an attempt to defraud a highly reputable company – in this case, Johnson & Johnson.

Implementing an action plan

As with other forms of PR crisis management, addressing the issue of fraud involves proven techniques and organizing an effective team that speaks with a single voice and responds promptly to inquiries. Countering the damage done by the perception of fraud by your client requires a plan of action that meets both short- and long-term goals. Short-term priorities of the crisis PR management team must include, as mentioned earlier, reliable fact-gathering, development of an internal and external communication plan, mobilization of supportive third parties who can vouch for the integrity of the firm, and development of a rapid response capability that enables the organization to set the story agenda rather than react to events and charges. Long term, the challenge is to remove any lingering doubts about the organization being committed to transparency and remaining worthy of the reputation it enjoyed before fraud became an issue.

The internal fact-finding process should include the company's most reliable and objective personnel supplemented, if necessary, by outsiders assigned by the crisis management team. The document they produce should be carefully reviewed by top management. It should be assembled in a straightforward readable form that takes responsibility for mistakes, apologizes if necessary, but does not appear defensive in tone.

Throughout, it is important to be sensitive to any human cost if fraud was involved. The crisis management team must make sure that if any individuals or organizations have suffered as a result of some wrongdoing, appropriate compensation or apologies are made and the public should be informed that these actions have been taken to address the problem.

PR crisis management requires an internal communication plan as well as an external plan directed at the larger public, so that the message is consistent and reinforced at every level. The internal plan must ensure that all key members of the organization are informed of the facts that have been gathered and the organization's message. A single spokesperson should be designated, whether it is a top executive of the firm or the PR consultancy, to deal with the issue of fraud. Once news organizations suspect that fraud is involved, they may try to speak to individuals in the accused company or to the victims to get another perspective. If all key personnel, including consultants who may work with the organization, are in the loop and working as a team, your message will come through with clarity.

Conclusion

Whenever fraud becomes an issue, the PR crisis management team must act with a sense of urgency appropriate to the high stakes that are involved in protecting or restoring an organization's reputation. Time is critical and each day that follows accusations of fraud or victimization by fraud should be treated as if the firm were promoting its side in a public referendum. A successful outcome requires a total commitment by all parties that have a stake in such a result. It is the challenge of the PR crisis management team to make that clear and use that sense of urgency to override inertia and take the necessary steps to protect or restore the organization's good reputation.

7 Reorganization and restructuring

Selling or closing a business – protecting reputation across national boundaries

Kathryn Tunheim (United States),
Marianne de Bruijn (The Netherlands)
and Jim Walsh (Ireland)

Introduction

The vast majority of transactions that change ownership of a business enterprise are completed over a period of time, with the consent of both buyer and seller – and as a result should be able to avoid most of the characteristics of other 'crisis situations'. Similarly, when a business closure is planned there is usually time to prepare for any communication needs.

The subset of transactions that comprise hostile take-overs do bear grim resemblance to other kinds of crisis environments: time pressures, incomplete information and tenuous information sources. Even in mutually agreeable merger and acquisition (M&A) transactions, however, there is a need to treat the shareholder audience as pre-eminent: it is there that the success or failure of the deal will ultimately be measured. This creates challenges for effective communication with all the other stakeholders. The need to communicate effectively to protect an organization's reputation is the same whether there is time to prepare, as in the examples in this chapter, or when a crisis strikes unexpectedly.

In today's world, reputation is not confined within national borders. Action in one country is very likely to have repercussions elsewhere in the world. Common to these examples of crisis management is the need for transnational communications, from the United States to Switzerland, across Denmark, Germany and France and from Ireland to Japan.

Swiss purchase of US financial services company

Kathryn Tunheim

Situation summary

A United States-based financial services company made a strategic decision to divest one of its signature business units. It was the division that had long symbolized the corporate brand. But as the industry had evolved, the company determined that it did not have the global scale to compete effectively, and sought to find the right acquirer to take full advantage of the talented people and strong client base of that unit. After a confidential sales process conducted by an investment bank, the winning bidder was a Swiss-based financial giant. Both buyer and seller were publicly traded companies, which meant that all communication considerations would be affected by the requirement to meet the disclosure guidelines of numerous financial exchanges.

Even as the sales solicitation process was under way, the communication executive of the selling organization began to lay out plans for an effective announcement, and the transition of the enterprise. Given the likelihood that the jobs of the internal communication staff of the US unit would be affected by the sale, it was decided to outsource the early planning efforts to protect confidentiality and objectivity.

Key considerations and risks included the following:

1. The value of the business being sold was very much dependent on the stability of the sales force across the United States: the continuity of client relations was more reliant on the stability of the field force than any other factor, including corporate ownership. So the field force needed to feel positively impacted by the transaction – even though it meant their employer was selling them!

2. Given both the needs of the field force and the tight time-frame that had to be managed, there were more than two dozen management executives who would need to be notified of the news, prepared to serve as spokespeople, and then be deployed into the field – all within a 48-hour period.
3. The acquiring company's executives understood the essential role that they needed to play: to highlight their enthusiasm for this acquisition. They literally needed to 'sell' the transaction to the field force of the acquired company within a very short time; it was understood that upon release of the news, competing financial services organizations would swoop and try to recruit the top field performers – and their customers.

Essential programme elements

A very frank layout of the goals and considerations for the communication effort was prepared and shared – first with the executives of the selling organization and, when appropriate, with the executives of the acquiring company. In the compressed timeline, it was critical that the top-level spokespeople had a clear and consistent definition of success: they would be faced with myriad decisions on-the-fly in the coming days, and would benefit from access to a common baseline for those decisions.

A comprehensive grid was developed and shared, identifying subsets of stakeholders, key messages for each subset and optimal vehicles for delivering those messages to each group. A timing-and-action plan was prepared and shared, making explicit each management office's role, and helping all involved understand how their role fitted into the overall effort. This also reinforced the essential need to honour the tight timeframe by highlighting the interdependency of various communication activities.

Draft materials were completed and approved through both companies by the outside public relations team, with plans to turn over all execution of the plan to the internal public relations staff as soon as the news became public. Internally, it was important to allow staff to show their professionalism under pressure; externally, it was optimal to highlight the capacity for business continuity to the media and analysts who would be clamouring to cover the story that first day. Materials included press releases, editorial backgrounders on each company, scripts for various levels of employee discussion, script for a security analysts' session and a Q&A.

Results

Negotiations on the final details of the transactions continued to the last moment, culminating over a weekend. In time for a pre-market announcement in Europe, the information crossed newswires around the world, and triggered the comprehensive plans already in the hands of communication and executive managers in both companies. Field office staff had customized information from their own managers by the time they arrived at their desks that Monday morning (and in many cases, had received electronic notification even earlier). By the end of the second day after the announcement, all staff of the acquired company had been in meetings with the leaders of both companies, security analysts had been briefed, community leaders in affected locations had been reached and media coverage was factual and supportive. Within months, the high retention of field staff and customers by the new ownership (and new brand identity) – along with strong stock performances for both companies – signalled a very successful M&A communication effort.

Moving business from The Netherlands to Germany

Marianne de Bruijn

In February 2006 the management of a French firm with 23 shops and a distribution centre in The Netherlands decided to move its entire distribution to Germany. The company had sold products in The Netherlands for many years. At the time of the reorganization about 90 per cent of all products were sold by distance selling, for example through the internet. The main reason for the reorganization was the overcapacity of the German distribution centre.

About 65 people were affected personally by the reorganization. Of this group 40 people worked in 'pick and pack' and 13 worked in data-entry. Most of the employees to be made redundant were women who worked part-time and were loyal to the company; 80–90 per cent of the people being dismissed did not have any qualifications. An estimated 15 per cent were non-Dutch.

The departments that did remain in The Netherlands were customer relations, finance and control, marketing departments and management (about 55 people). The aim of the firm was to reorganize the distribution in such a way that the customers would not notice any change or disruption.

Reasons and risks

The Dutch division of the company had produced good results over the past years. It was not a question of bringing the operation into profitability but more an issue of logistics profitability at a European level. In a stagnating European context, big groups have to restructure to maintain and improve their competitiveness. The distribution centre had to be moved to Germany because the Dutch plant was not large enough to absorb the German activity; the German site was chosen to absorb the Dutch activities.

Within the company there had been a long-term market decline for The Netherlands operation. Many players were picking up in the market in 2005. In The Netherlands the firm and its brand were losing market share because the brand seemed to be a little old-fashioned for Dutch consumers. To make the brand more appealing, there had to be investment in the internet and a drive to improve awareness and attractiveness.

The reorganization happened in parallel with another development within the firm, namely the closing of several shops in The Netherlands. Eventually the plan was to keep only seven to eight shops – out of 23 in total – in the large cities in The Netherlands. The reason for closing the other shops was the fierce competition and rising costs. Shop density is much higher in The Netherlands than in the surrounding countries, leading to scarcity and rising rents, especially in the most preferred locations. In 2005 the company had experienced varying fortunes with its shops, in particular some of them encountered very difficult trading. In December 2005, franchisees had been informed about these developments and were offered the chance to terminate their contracts.

Another market development was that many other companies were reorganizing their activities in 2006. Beiersdorf in The Netherlands dismissed 170 out of 240 employees. At NedCar

1,000 jobs disappeared and Neckermann dismissed another 100. Employees of these firms held several strikes and the media covered every one of them. These developments increased sensitivity about the reorganization of the French firm.

Media relations and results

During the closing of some franchise shops there was negative publicity in the local media. The company wanted to avoid similar negative publicity during the reorganization and to achieve this the management in France and The Netherlands wanted to be transparent in the whole process.

ACA/JES Communicatie was asked to develop a range of communication tools for the firm to act quickly in case of a crisis. Together with the French IPREX agency Beau Fixe, an official statement about the collective redundancies and Q&A documents were prepared in case of leaks to the media through employees, the works council or trade unions.

Financial information was prepared for the Centre for Work and Income (CWI) and the trade unions. The company helped the redundant personnel by setting up a social plan that all parties (management, works council and unions) agreed upon. They prepared a document to inform the employees, which was open about the financial situation of the firm and the necessity for the decision. Employees were fully supported on leaving the firm and in finding new jobs. Affected employees were pleased with the treatment and press rumours about the reorganization never materialized.

Given this lack of media interest, ACA/JES and the management of the firm decided not to send out any press releases, but to be prepared to react swiftly if necessary. The works council was very professional and hired a mediator to mediate between itself and the management team. This worked really well for all parties involved. Even when local journalists visited the firm to cover a story about a prize winner, it did not cross anyone's mind to discuss the reorganization with them. There were no strikes.

The closing of the distribution centre eventually took place at the beginning of December. Shops were closed during 2006. The results of the reorganization were positive for the company. Distribution was taken over by Germany and costs were reduced and distribution was more effective. Affected employees were helped by the Centre of Work and Income to find new jobs and many of them, especially the younger people, quickly found new ones.

When communication is open and transparent during the whole process of a reorganization, the people affected are more likely to respond in a positive way.

Goodwill is vital in a closure situation

Jim Walsh

Goodwill and a solid reputation for effective communication are vital when bad news has to be given.

Announcing the closure of a plant employing 350, which has been operating in a small community for 30 years, is not easy. When faced with that task early in 2006, the management of NEC Semiconductors Ireland did what they had done for 30 years: they considered the effect on their workers to be a priority and developed a communication programme to reflect that concern.

The decision to close was not a local one. It was made by NEC Electronics Corporation, the Semiconductor's parent company in Tokyo; and it was made for sound business reasons. The company operated a number of similar plants around the world, in mainland Europe, Asia and the United States. The Irish plant was the smallest and the international trading dimension of the business, plus the scale of the plant, made it impossible to achieve the level of operating costs required. NEC Electronics was stepping up its cost-cutting measures to improve financial performance following a forecast of group operating losses for the fiscal year ending 31 March 2006.

On a stand-alone basis the Irish management and employees had been working hard to improve efficiency and at the same time produce to the quality levels demanded in the marketplace. In the two years before closure, the plant had managed to turn in a small profit each year, but it was carrying losses from previous years, which clearly would not be recoverable.

Ballivor in County Meath, the site of the NEC plant for 30 years, is a small village about 30 miles north-west of Ireland's capital city, Dublin. With the development of Dublin's infrastructure and the rapid rise in property prices in the city, villages like Ballivor were growing rapidly as more people had to move outside the immediate Dublin area to find affordable homes. The bulk of the 350 employees at NEC Semiconductors in Ballivor came from within a 30-mile radius of the plant, with a core group of longer serving staff from the village itself.

In drawing up its communication plan to announce the closure, the NEC management had a number of issues to consider. First was the need to ensure that no public announcement was made and no information leaked before the staff had been informed. Second, it was also important to notify the Irish Government and the state bodies who had encouraged NEC to come to Ireland in 1976 and who had supported the company in the initial years through generous inward investment programmes. These programmes have resulted in Ireland attracting virtually all of the leading technical and pharma companies to set up manufacturing plants in the country. Intel, HP, Dell, Pfizer, Wyeth and many similar businesses have provided a strong base for the economic prosperity enjoyed by Ireland over the past 15 to 20 years. Third, there were Tokyo Stock Exchange regulations to consider as the NEC Semiconductor parent company was a listed company.

A programme was prepared involving local senior managers with the aid of external IR and PR support with experience of similar situations. The announcement day, 21 February 2006, was selected based on the objectives listed above and a schedule of activities prepared leading to that day. Media information, Q&As and backgrounders were all prepared and signed off by management in Ireland and Tokyo.

The timing of the announcement was problematic as the plant worked three shifts around the clock. It was agreed that the announcement should be made at 4 pm on a Tuesday so that those coming off the second shift and those reporting for the third shift would all be on the premises. This left one shift to be included, which operated from 11 pm to 7 am. It was decided that workers on that shift should be requested to return to the plant following their shift for a company announcement regarding its future. Advance notice of the meeting was also given to the workers representatives, SIPTU (Services Industrial Professional Technical Union) and government agencies and representatives.

The nature of the announcement was not revealed to the workers, but announcing the meeting seven hours in advance meant that the period from 7 am until 4 pm became the most critical time in terms of media leaks. Anticipating that the media would be informed of the meeting during this period proved to be correct. Within hours of the meeting being announced calls were received at the plant from local media. One of the calls was from a local freelance journalist who was a 'stringer' for some of the national media, which quickly followed up on the breaking story.

All media calls were routed to the external public relations consultant who was able to confirm that a meeting was being held but not its nature. He was, however, able to provide background information on the company and its contribution to the Irish economy and the local community.

Although the workers at the plant were prepared for a major announcement there was still shock at the meeting when they were told of the decision to close. As the meeting was in progress, a full statement was issued to the local and national media, most of whom had sent journalists and reporters to the plant.

Following the meeting the Managing Director, Kenji Yamashiro, and the Company Secretary, Joe Carroll, held a press conference in the grounds of the plant for the media and outlined the reasons and the timetable for closure. Interviews were also conducted with trade union officials and employees leaving the meeting. The overwhelming message that came from these interviews was that closure was a result of global market conditions and not from the way the plant was managed or the quality of the work. There were also vivid television pictures of workers saying that while they were obviously shocked and disappointed they paid tribute to the company as being 'a great place to work'.

The announcement in February gave the end of September as the final closure date. Immediately after the announcement, the company began negotiations with staff representatives and instigated an outplacement programme that provided for many different staff needs. The programme provided support in preparing CVs and facilitated a job fair, set up in the plant, where companies seeking people with the skills used in NEC Semiconductors could interview prospective staff. Seminars in money management were arranged to help people see the opportunities to use the cash that would be coming from their redundancy payments. Those who wished to retrain for a new skill or to set up in business were provided with skills and business training opportunities.

While assisting employees to prepare for the change in their lives, the programme was also important in helping to maintain morale while the logistics of closing down were being implemented. It is a credit to the management and workforce that the closure went so smoothly. No customer order missed its deadline and the machinery at the plant was moved seamlessly to other NEC Electronic plants overseas.

The final chapter in the closure of NEC Semiconductors at Ballivor was concluded in the same spirit of openness and dignity with which the company had conducted its business over the previous 30 years. Formal calls were made to the Irish Government to thank the state bodies that had assisted the company in setting up and operating.

Two formal events were held on 29 and 30 September 2006. On Friday 29 September, when work was completed, a closure event was held for staff and representatives from the local community. This culminated in the lowering of the Irish, Japanese and company flags from outside the premises. During the event a number of speeches were made by former and current employees, employee representatives and local community representatives. Extracts from these speeches give a glimpse of the goodwill that the company had accumulated and the esteem in which it was held.

Theresa Shaw, one of the first workers in the plant in 1976 said: 'We are thankful for the quality of life we have enjoyed from being employed by this company. NEC you have served us well.'

Sean Gunning, who had been with NEC for 27 years, recounted meeting a reporter some time after the closure announcement in February. The reporter told Sean that it was remarkable that 'despite all the people they had in the factory, they couldn't find one single employee to say anything bad about NEC'.

A former HR manager, Justin Wallace, described the feelings in the company towards the Japanese management and staff who had come to Ballivor to work at various periods over the years: 'They will always be remembered here with respect and affection.'

Worker representative John Regan of SIPTU said that the way the closure was handled was unique: 'There won't be another in this country so well run or brought to a satisfactory conclusion for everybody. I believe that the package that was put together was fair and reasonable and very good for the workers.'

Ballivor school principal William Keegan echoed the affection for NEC in the community and outlined many of the community initiatives undertaken by the company.

The following evening, Saturday 30 September, a more social event was held for employees and their partners in a local hotel. More than 500 people attended, including the Japanese Ambassador to Ireland, Keiichi Hayashi, and the Irish Minister for Communications, Noel Dempsey, TD, who lives in the area.

Key to achieving a smooth and uncritical closure was the fact that the company behaved with concern for its employees and customers, as it had consistently done throughout its history. This concern was reflected in the communication programme and the detailed approach to alerting all stakeholders in an appropriate fashion. As a result there were no premature media stories. The company message was presented fully and accurately and was therefore completely understood.

The legacy of NEC Semiconductors in Ballivor, County Meath, will live through a number of initiatives. It supported a local group, 'Next Era Calling' set up to seek an alternative industry for the site. It also donated funds to have a disused church converted into a public library in the village, and to the work of Equal Ireland to help fund its BA degree in Humanities in the Workplace and Community Practice. The donation to both of these projects was the final act of the company as it closed its doors.

Conclusion

The M&A and closure activities described here had a strong level of media interest. More important, they also demonstrate the importance of direct communication with other key audiences, including employees and customers.

A common thread in each story is the degree of goodwill that existed for the companies involved prior to the events described. The level of trust and support for a company faced with a crisis is determined by its behaviour and way of communicating over a period of time.

Consistency in communication helps build confidence and preserve an organization's reputation at a time when it needs it most. It is also crucial that that consistency is maintained when a crisis happens. When dealing with a crisis, any attempt to position your organization in a way that is alien to its normal behaviour will expose it to ridicule and charges of insincerity.

8 A multitude of challenges for the international food sector

Why all food companies should adopt proactive planning and communication strategies to deal with crises

Mania Xenou (Greece) and
Nuria Sánchez (Spain)

The international food industry is a dynamic, competitive and high-profile sector that plays a key role in global financial development. However, the food industry is currently confronted with a multitude of challenges that have led it to be the most crisis-prone sector. Two of the major challenges faced by the industry and by consumers are the safety of food and the dialogue on the impact of diet on our life and health.

In recent years, it has become increasingly possible for crises to occur in the food industry, due to intensified primary production. Constantly rising demand around the world, creating the need for increased and intensive production, means that some businesses have struggled to survive and have cut costs on controls and safety procedures in an attempt to remain competitive. This has sometimes led to fatal results.

Nowadays the international food industry has to defend itself on a daily basis both for the quality and safety of the food supplied to consumers, and for the eating habits it has encouraged. It has to deal with a suspicious public and troubled consumers. In this context the food industry is probably going through the most critical period it has ever faced. The media are critical and the financial costs are huge. It is a complex and uncertain environment and it comes as no surprise that the food industry is one of the most regulated.

Food safety

Food crises around the world, coupled with the power of the media, have created suspicious and demanding consumers and a growing number of consumer organizations. State governments and other authorities have enacted and enforced new regulations for the industry, responding to incidents such as mad cow disease and dioxins, which had dire social, economic and political consequences.

Mad cow disease (1996) is a typical example of a food crisis with wide-ranging economic effects. The market for British beef fell by 30 per cent within two days, as consumers turned their backs on beef, even in countries that had no experience of the disease. Within a few days after the crisis emerged, prices dropped by 50 per cent in France, and the demand for beef fell 30 to 35 per cent in Germany, 60 per cent in Greece, 40 per cent in Portugal, 30 per cent in Spain, and 25 per cent in Italy. France and Belgium banned imports of British beef and Germany pressed for a ban throughout the European Union (EU).

China, which did not import British beef, issued emergency measures to stop contaminated meat entering the country. In New Zealand, the Ministry of Health withdrew all British beef products from supermarkets and shops. Australia's health minister urged people to remove any products made from British beef from their cupboards. On 26 March 1996 the EU imposed a ban on Britain's beef exports that was not lifted until 10 years later, in March 2006. The ban had a tremendous economic and social impact in the UK.

The dioxin contamination, which started in Belgium in 1999, also had serious consequences. Within two to three weeks after the crisis was announced, at least 30 countries including Canada, Australia, Hong Kong, Taiwan, Russia, Egypt, Algeria, Poland, South Africa and most European states banned imports of Belgian agricultural products and removed Belgian products from the shelves. The United States and Singapore banned all European poultry and pork.

The information that contaminated feed had been given inadvertently to cattle and pigs led the EU to order the destruction of those animals at around 1,000 farms. The Food Industry Federation of Belgium (FEVIA) estimated that 6,000 people were out of a job and US $750 million was lost as result of the crisis. A report from the Belgian government stated that the cost of the dioxin crisis to the food industry was US $1.54 billion, half within the agricultural sector and half in other food industry sectors.

Health and diet issues

Health issues related to obesity, which is at epidemic proportions around the world, forced the European and US authorities to take measures to fight the problem.

Being severely overweight or obese is a risk factor in many chronic diseases and premature death. The EU called upon member states to conceive and implement initiatives aimed at promoting healthy diets and physical activity. A ground-breaking example was the announcement made by the European Platform for Action on Dietary, Physical Activity and Health Issues. This EU initiative was presented in detail by Markos Kyprianos during the open session of FHFI's Annual General Meeting in March 2006.

Multinational food companies have joined the European Commission's drive to fight obesity in Europe. They have developed programmes such as McDonalds' Nutrition Information Initiative, and have stopped advertising certain foods to children under 12. Members of UNESDA (the soft drinks manufacturers association, represented by Coca-Cola and Pepsi) and Unilever, are reformulating their products, and Kraft Foods is not marketing products directly to children unless they meet a certain nutritional profile. The first official reaction to the problem of obesity and nutrition came from France, which has established rules whereby all advertisements for food and drink in France must carry healthy eating messages; non-complying companies will face fines.

Crisis preparation is the key to success

The food industry, both the primary and the commercial sector, is active in the implementation of crisis management procedures. It is well versed in difficult situations, due to the vast number of food issues and the frequency with which they occur (GMOs, dioxins, mad cow disease, avian influenza, trans fats, acrylamids, antibiotics, etc). Consumers are increasingly conscious of food safety and nutrition issues, frequently raising issues of their own.

Food companies as well as government bodies must protect consumers and society in general from food risks by developing crisis management systems, well-trained specialists and safety systems. Food companies must provide for a wide range of risks, especially in the fields of toxicology, microbiology, analytical chemistry, product and service design, and the safety and protection of life and the environment.

Crisis management requires thorough preparation on the part of food companies. They need to start with a simple organizational plan and set up a crisis management group which, following constant training and practice on a wide range of risks and possible scenarios, will be able to manage the crises.

The group should be trained to ensure that accurate information is gathered to help in the proper assessment of risks and enable dispassionate decision making in ways that do not interfere with the smooth operation of the company. The successful handling of an imminent risk requires the ability to predict crises, to assess the risk and threat, and to build a constructive dialogue with the public.

The lack of proactive crisis management in the food industry can have far-reaching, even tragic results. It is not just business activity that is at risk: it can also affect jobs, the company's reputation, physical safety and loss of life. And, as we have seen with dioxins and mad cow disease, it can even lead to a global food crisis.

Stakeholders

The food sector is crisis prone and requires the use of all communication tools and much stakeholder involvement.

Food crisis communication has to deal with different groups with different agendas and priorities. Consumers, consumer groups, the media, the industry, states and authorities, NGOs, academics, scientists, business and social partners are all parties involved in this public debate. Crisis communications must be based on clear and accurate messages that target the different needs and interests of different stakeholders.

The times when each food company made decisions without reference to others are long gone. The industry prepares and markets products with which consumers identify. Food products are directly related to the identity and development of people and it is quite reasonable for different categories of citizens/consumers to ask questions every time a nutrition issue comes up. The industry must take seriously the views and needs all parties involved in this dialogue and learn to communicate with them within a crisis communication protocol.

The need for proactive communication

The international food industry is facing a range of critical issues on food safety, health and nutrition. Debates over these issues lead to everyday crises that demand decisive action through crisis communication.

The public's concerns are multiplied by the power of the media. The media have become more active in their reporting, having more news communication tools in their hands. They are sometimes responsible for creating a climate of fear over food safety.

Understandably, consumers demand certainty that their food supply is safe. Despite the flare-up of crises, science and modern technology have made our food safer and risk has been reduced. This is the most important fact for the food industry to communicate.

Proactive communication with clear and uncomplicated messages can gain public trust and avoid rumours and speculation. Clear identification of the audience, trusted sources and an effective strategy for dealing with the media are necessary to successfully communicate on the issues that the industry is dealing with.

The media

Food safety and hygiene are covered on an almost daily basis by the print and broadcast media. Food and nutrition in general are particularly attractive subjects for the media and their audiences, because the public's fears and concerns are never far from the surface. The public's interest can lead to emotionally-charged coverage of food issues, which attracts many more readers and television viewers.

With the internet and other communication tools, the global diffusion of information is rapid. It takes only a few minutes for news to travel around the world. This speed and the nature of the internet can, however, guarantee neither the validity of the source nor the authority of the information. This can lead to unfounded, or at least incorrect, information being spread on important and sensitive issues, including the safety of certain foods.

The modern media, including the internet, frequently report news regarding food safety and hygiene in a simplistic way that can terrify and alarm consumers. The traditional media often assume an aggressive stance on issues relating to the food industry. But their views cannot be verified by consumers and they end up totally confused and uncertain when buying food in supermarkets, restaurants and market stalls. Nevertheless, we should stress the contribution the media make in exposing the many food-related scandals which would not have come to light but for their reports.

All this can only lead to the conclusion that the food industry, the state and the media must provide accurate and well-founded information. Accurate information will protect consumers from false and inaccurate reports, and financial risks and major crises will be avoided.

Conclusion

Modern society is caught in a pendulum effect with regard to anything that has to do with food. The constant food crises and their important financial and political consequences have set the limits inside which the food sector moves. These are the narrow limits of a pendulum which swings from one side to the other within a crisis-oriented environment, in a continuous attempt to limit the risk it runs. There is a supply and demand information system, which also sets the boundaries of the crises-oriented communication environment for food.

Consumers rightly demand specific information about the food they consume. The industry, as well as governments, must meet this demand by supplying suitable and accurate information. The correct balance between the supply of and demand for information is necessary to help consumers make informed choices, trusting the information provided to them. This accurate information balance will help us escape this pendulum effect in which we are all caught.

Case study: an example of food, ecological, political and social crisis – the sinking of the *Prestige*

Nuria Sánchez (Spain)

On 13 November 2002, at 14:50, the oil tanker *Prestige* broadcast an appeal for help in Cape Finisterre (Galicia, Spain). It was carrying 77,000 tons of fuel oil and it had suffered a breakdown and was adrift. The ship's crew was successfully rescued, but the Spanish authorities discovered a fuel leak at sea.

The ship, built in 1976, was leaving a large slick of oil in its wake. The *Prestige*, sailing under the Bahamas flag, was serving the route Latvia–Singapore and should have been taken out of service long ago. The results of the spill were devastating: 2,000 kilometres of coast were polluted by the black tide; fishing was prohibited in a 486 kilometre area and the whole seafood industry faced a serious risk of collapse. It is a good example of an ecological and political catastrophe as well as a food and social crisis.

After a week of breakdowns and problems, the *Prestige* finally sank on 20 November 2002. The sinking and its consequences became a cover story in both the Spanish and international media. The government of the time, el Partido Popular, was not responsible for the accident, but was guilty in the eyes of the world's public opinion. Why? Because it reacted late to the crisis and in such a clumsy way that it seemed responsible, giving opposition parties the opportunity to make a connection between the most serious ecological disaster ever suffered in Spain and one of the most notorious sinkings ever, and the government's poor communication.

Figure 8.1 The *Prestige* in the sea

An administration under fire

Beyond the serious mistakes committed in the political-administrative management of the accident (underestimation of the problem, delayed reaction), the truth is that the Spanish government did not know how to tackle the crisis in terms of handling the media.

It did not establish a single, authoritative information point, which is crucial in crisis situations; the Portuguese

Hydrographical Institute and the French Prevention Institute acted as the main initial information referents for the catastrophe. The Spanish remained silent, did not react and no one from the government appeared at the start of the crisis to give an official version of the facts, the action plan adopted, etc. It allowed others to take the initiative and the main opposition party announced measures and votes of no confidence while the president of the Galician government was away hunting, far from the accident.

Underestimating the catastrophe

Days after the accident, the government was overwhelmed by events, and an unstoppable black tide marched menacingly towards one of the richest coasts in Spain. It was a secondary representative of the local government – and not the President himself – who had to respond to public opinion. Too late! By then, almost everybody had made up their own mind about the problem. The representative and his team of speakers devoted their time to minimizing the problem:

> All the fuel that has been heading for the coast has already arrived there. (Enrique L[oacute] pez Veiga, Fishing Councillor of the Galician local government, 17 November 2002.)

> At a guess, the ship could have lost between 3,000 and 4,000 tons of fuel. (Arsenio Fernández de Mesa, government delegate in Galicia, 19 November 2002.) He fell short by 73,000 tons.

> This is by no means a black tide. There are just some very localized minor spills. (Mariano Rajoy, Vice President of the Spanish government, 23 November 2002.)

Different criteria for action

There were different criteria for action. While the maritime Captain of La Coruña was asserting that tugging the vessel to the north was not sensible, the Minister for Public Works declared that he was for taking it as far as possible from the Spanish coast.

Short sightedness and excess of confidence

The government did not realize the extent of the problem and was not able to satisfy the media's 'information hunger'. The media began searching for any information on their own, through their own sources, recording on-the-spot the images of thousands of volunteers cleaning up the coast and their lack of equipment; fishermen showing contaminated fish to the cameras; and voices of alarm announcing the consequences this tragedy would have for a fishing industry that not only supplies fish and seafood to Spain, but also to countries such as France, Italy and Germany. And again, the government took a wrong turn – self-justification: 'I cannot remember such an informative intensity at a government's level in quality, transparency and in real time as this is' (Francisco Áblvarez Cascos, Minister of Public Works, 6 November 2002).

Figure 8.2 People cleaning the coast

What was happening was not considered important. The President of the Autonomous Regional Government, Manuel Fraga, was out hunting; the Minister's whereabouts were unknown; and President Aznar did not even consider visiting Galicia until 14 December. Instead of travelling to the disaster area to have his picture taken with the fuel spill at his back, President Aznar preferred to appear on television in an interview granted to the chief editor of the Spanish public TV informative services. Even then, instead of starting by apologizing, he accused the opposition party of using the calamity for political gain.

In sum, the government found itself overwhelmed by events and, performing an exercise in 'informative autism', was led to the dock where public opinion passed sentence on the executive.

Figure 8.3 Sea bird after the accident

Many lessons can be learnt from the *Prestige* catastrophe:

- It had a serious impact on politics, food industry security, environmental protection, public opinion and the political stability of the country.
- Many interested parties were involved: politicians, food safety agents, ecologists and so on.
- The crisis was developed and followed through the media and the internet, 24/7, using mass media techniques, and the audience determined who was the guilty party.

Such a serious scenario required new solutions: a communication strategy and a plan from the start, a unique management and dialogue team, and an accurate evaluation of the accident and its consequences. It should have been an exercise in paying attention to the affected people and public opinion. None of that was done. A year after the events, coinciding with the first anniversary of the catastrophe, the Minister for Promotion of the Government published a report, 'Ministry of Public Works. Achievements on maritime security and the fight against pollution in the past year'. It was too late.

9 Negative press and how to deal with it

No ostriches need apply

Elizabeth Seigenthaler Courtney
(United States) and Willem Buitelaar
(The Netherlands)

Introduction

Suddenly and often without warning, it happens. The company or organization that you have managed, cultivated and cared for is under scrutiny by an unforgiving journalist or group of reporters.

Negative coverage may result from a very public incident that shines a harsh spotlight on your company's operations or practices. Or it may be caused by an investigation of a corporate practice. Or perhaps your organization is under scrutiny by a government agency or involved in contentious litigation that leads to damaging news.

Regardless of the reason for the coverage, negative news – whether a singular article or a seemingly endless series of print, electronic and broadcast stories – can cause long-term damage to your company's reputation and hence its financial performance. This is especially true during this age of electronic communication when even stories that appear on minor news outlets can have a long and healthy life on the internet or can instantaneously be forwarded to hundreds of people whether they are your customers, your competitors or your shareholders.

Negative news stings, because you care about your company and its reputation. Often, when derogatory news hits, your first concern is for those who know you best of all – how will your employees feel? What will your family think? How does this look to your business associates, neighbours or friends? The very personal nature of these questions leads to the often-precarious way that executives react to negative news coverage. Business is personal and any attack on your business seems like a personal attack. The natural response is to react personally and, hence, defensively. On the flip side, a well-conceived, appropriate and strategic response to negative news can mitigate damages while paving the way for your organization's complete recovery.

Prepare early and often

First, regardless of the size or purpose of your organization, always be prepared for the possibility of negative news coverage. If you are open for business, you may be subject to media scrutiny at some point. Just as you plan for your company's continuity in the event of a physical disaster, prepare to manage your organization's reputation through a period of negative news coverage related to a crisis. Several important steps include:

- Make certain that your company has sound financial, human resource and operational policies and that employees at every level of the company understand them. Errors that create crises sometimes occur, yet many of the most serious incidents are preventable with sound policies, rigorously enforced.
- Determine who in your organization will serve as a spokesperson. This person should be in a management or public relations role and be calm and articulate.
- Ensure that this individual has appropriate media training. Find an independent coach who can help you anticipate tough questions and your company's response *before* the negative coverage occurs.
- Prepare professional and factual materials that define your company. Always have a current company profile or fact sheet that details your organization's mission, philosophy and executive team. This information should also be posted on your website.
- Get to know the media outlets that cover your organization. These include local news and business outlets in the community in which your company is based and industry trade publications. Subscribe to those publications and follow their coverage of your community's businesses or your industry.
- Get personally acquainted with the media personnel in your area. Take the time to invite reporters from your community to get to know your company. The more they understand your business now, the more accurate their coverage will be when your company is under scrutiny.

Mitigate impact with proactive response

Second, consider that in most cases you are likely to know that unfavourable news is coming *before* the first article appears. Journalists should give you the opportunity to respond, in advance of the story's publication, to any affront to your company. Legitimate journalists operate within a well-developed code of ethics regulated by organizations such as the US Society of Professional Journalists (www.spj.org). Examples of the types of tenets upheld by this professional group include:

- seek truth and report it;
- minimize harm;
- act independently;
- be accountable.

It is important to recognize these and other journalistic standards because, if you are the target of a negative news story, reporters should uphold these principles. If they fail to do so, you may seek the involvement of the publication's management, request corrections or pursue legal action.

One important guideline for journalists is that the subject of a story should never be surprised by its content. The reporter should contact you and give you the opportunity to offer comment regarding every negative accusation or slight against your company before the story appears. This response is your first opportunity to manage your way through negative news coverage and it should never be ignored.

The best way to formulate such a response is as follows:

- Involve top leadership. The chief executive and other principals of the firm must be involved in the decision-making process, defining the company's position and the development of the message.
- Do the right thing. If your company has done something wrong or created a problem for someone else, work to right the situation in the way that you treat employees, customers or neighbours. This may cost the company money and time, but it can also help you to maintain your reputation. Tangible actions speak volumes and will take you far in your efforts to control the damage resulting from negative incidents.
- Understand that your first reaction is important and will shape your future relationship with the media and the credibility of your image with the public. Any reporter who calls should get a return phone call, and every response to a journalist should be well formulated.

- Before calling the reporter, get all the facts about the incident in question. Your knowledge, and hence your response, is only as good as your information.
- Involve your legal counsel. Frequently there is tension between the legal and public relations responses. However, protecting the company from a legal perspective is crucial, especially during a time of crisis. Attorneys should have the opportunity to collaborate with the communication team to determine a reasonable approach in developing a media strategy.
- Determine your key messages and fully develop them. This is a crucial step. Evaluate words carefully and test them internally. Consider how they will come across to your customers, to other businesses and to opinion leaders.
- Release the bad news all at once. Whether you have a series of job lay-offs, or numbers of people near death due to food poisoning at your restaurant, it is not wise to try to minimize the impact by letting the news dribble out over time. A huge one-day story has a shorter-term impact than a drawn-out string of articles that snow-ball over days, weeks or months. Don't think that all or part of the bad news can be contained – eventually it will get out.
- Evaluate the media outlet in question and its credibility. Understand its reach, audience and journalistic style.
- Research the reporter and read his or her previous work. Is he or she experienced? How fairly has he or she covered previous issues? Is there cause for concern because of his or her approach?
- If you decide to move forward with an interview, decide who the best spokesperson is. Make this determination based on the gravity of the situation. Often, minor incidents can be handled by a communication professional, while interviews involving more serious issues should be handled by top management.
- Anticipate likely questions and company responses. These questions and responses should be committed to writing. Think about the tough questions and determine any areas that you will not address.
- Depending upon the situation, decide whether to do a personal interview or whether to respond in a more controlled manner. Often, personal discussions are the best course of action. This is especially true in cases where a human voice can add the appropriate credibility, tone or explanation for the situation. However, if your company is under severe scrutiny, it may be advisable to prepare a controlled statement whereby you provide a response but are not subjected to a verbal inquisition by the journalist.
- Depending on the nature of the interview, you may ask to respond to the questions in writing. This provides a more controlled method of developing your organization's position.

- Practise your interview. Make certain that you convey a calm tone and professional demeanour regardless of the interrogatory skills of the reporter.
- Give the reporter a context before he or she launches into an interview. Often, the journalist will begin the discussion based on the facts, as he or she perceives them. It is also the journalist's obligation to hear what you have to say. Begin the interview with: 'Before you ask your questions, I'd like to give you some background about our company, its history and its approach.' You could provide information that includes your record of safety or customer service. Then emphasize key points that may give the journalist more context for the story.
- Always be truthful in your responses. It is better to refrain from comment than to say something that is not true. And don't be afraid to say, 'I don't know the answer to that question, but I'll find out.'
- Feel free to be assertive. If there is a key point that you want to convey – push for that. 'Please quote me as saying that we will investigate this matter to its fullest extent' or, 'It is important to me that you report that our company wants to express our deepest sympathy to the family of our employee who lost his life', are certainly appropriate requests.
- Never say 'No comment', which sounds abrupt and defensive. If you are unable to comment, you could say, 'Due to the nature of this litigation, if would be inappropriate for us to comment at this time' or, 'I can't provide you with a response because of proprietary issues, but I can tell you that our company is committed to the safety of every employee.'
- Never go 'off the record'. Recognize that nothing is truly off the record and that anything that you provide to a reporter can be used by him or her at some point.
- If appropriate, refer the reporter to others who will document your company's record or reputation. Whether they are industry experts, board members or customers, independent sources can add third-party credibility to a complex story.

Detecting a negative story before it appears

Even after you have gone through the correct preparations, some articles will slam your organization. If, after proactive preparation, you think that a story may be negative, there are ways to detect just how serious the issue will be in advance of publication. Assessing the severity of a story can help you to counteract its impact. You can spot a particularly negative story by:

- The type of questions that reporters ask your company. Are they investigative in nature? Are the reporters relying on other sources? Do they cite comments that others have made about your company – on or off the record? Have they researched previous coverage about your organization or asked to see documents?
- The numbers of times that the reporter calls you. Does he or she call back to check facts? Do the calls come over a series of days or weeks? The more time expended by the reporter, the more significant you can expect the story to be.
- Has the reporter called others to dig more deeply? If your directors, shareholders or customers have also been questioned, the story is likely to be less than positive.

If you perceive that a negative story is coming up, it is essential to examine the potential impact and plan a response before the story appears. The first step is to consider the reach of the news outlet. Who is likely to read or watch a negative story in this publication or on this channel? Is it a weekly newspaper or the *International Herald Tribune*? Is it likely to be a one-day news story or a series of stories? Is it a piece that will appear during prime time newscasts and be recounted on the internet, or is it for a targeted trade article? Once the story breaks, is it likely to spawn follow-up coverage from other outlets?

Understanding the parameters of the coverage and the credibility of the outlet will enable you to appropriately assess the extent to which you should respond to audiences of utmost importance.

No ostriches need apply

Once you recognize that a negative story is clearly being developed, don't put your head in the sand – as tempting as that response may seem at the time. Before a negative story breaks, a lack of action always seems to be the most attractive course. It's tempting to wait and see just how bad the story is or to hope and pray that the whole mess will go away somehow. Instead, carefully assess the potential impact of the coverage and then consider a possible course of action by:

- Determining and then communicating meaningful actions. Again, your company's efforts to make amends or fix a problem can take you far in fostering goodwill in a difficult situation. Even if you have to admit errors, that is sometimes better than ignoring a group or situation. Build confidence by setting a proactive course of action and then articulating that to the media and key audiences.

- If appropriate, request a meeting with the management of the news organization. If you have attempted to cooperate with the reporter but sense that you are not getting your message across, pursue a meeting with the management of the publication before the story breaks to make certain that your facts are being understood and conveyed.

- Once you know that a bad story will run, communicate with your close audiences in advance of its publication. Examples may be employees, customers, board members and shareholders. Decide if you want to notify any or all of these groups that a potential story is being developed and articulate the issues to be raised and the company response. The key is to maintain control of the message. This will prevent important audiences from being blindsided and enable them to be armed with the company response. If you decide to do this, avoid e-mail communication.

- Consider working with another, competing outlet to get your story across. If one news group has a bias against your company and you know that a negative story is coming, contact a competing publication that will be more open to your side of the story. This strategy can significantly defuse the negative piece, especially if the article that you plan appears first.

- Prepare communication for key groups to be distributed as soon as the story appears. Review the article and determine how you will react. This may include sending a letter to key audiences, posting a response on your website, or calling important customers to advise them of your company's response.

- Prepare company employees for an onslaught of calls from customers, vendors or others. Develop an internal routing system for calls and decide who will respond and how. Make certain that the person chosen is prepared with talking points.

- Prepare for other news outlets to call. Journalists follow one another with coverage. Make certain that you are prepared to respond to other reporters who will pick up the story once it appears. Maintain consistent messages throughout your communication with journalists.

- Pull objective sources into interviews. If you have customers, shareholders or business associates who will vouch for your company's integrity, it may be helpful to suggest that reporters interview these people.

Depending upon the incident and your reaction, negative coverage can be a one-day news story with minimal impact; or it can go on and on, spiralling into more serious and long-term damage.

Building bridges toward recovery

Regardless of how long-term or short-lived the coverage is, it is important to build bridges with important audiences, especially if your credibility has suffered. After you have survived a barrage of bad coverage, your organization can reconstruct its image in the following ways:

- Survey key groups. Conduct professional quantitative or qualitative research to gauge the impact of the damage on your employees, customers or shareholders.
- Develop a series of long-term objectives based on recovery. Establish measurable goals that respond to recurring issues. Objectives could include rebuilding employee morale, re-establishing market share, or cementing the reputation in the community.
- Focus on core audiences with strategic programmes and outreach. Demonstrate your willingness to listen to key groups and respond to their issues with a series of targeted strategies. Whether it involves outreach programmes, or focused communication materials, this will require the consistent repetition of messages.
- Maintain positive positioning of the company by developing advertisements and editorial coverage within publications that are important to your audiences. If your organization upholds a sustained level of paid visibility and positive media coverage, a balanced perspective emerges, which means that the impact of negative coverage is not as severe or long-term.
- Measure the planned objectives to ensure successful recovery.

Conclusion

A crisis or other issues that lead to negative news about your organization can be an excruciating experience. However, many credible companies have recovered and gone on to soar once again following a seemingly catastrophic torrent of negative news. Your ability to recover is directly tied to your ability to plan and communicate proactively. Every organization can make mistakes or be subject to scrutiny. But, ultimately, lessons in business mirror lessons in life. It is not what happens to you, it is how you handle it that makes the difference.

Case study

The picture beside the zoom lens or how to reduce the impact on the image abroad of flooding in a country – damage control in the Low Countries
Willem Buitelaar (The Netherlands)

It happened in January 1995. Due to torrential rain in the north of France and in Germany, The Netherlands risked – and partly experienced – a significant flood. During late January and the early days of February an important part of the country risked being covered with water and other parts were inundated. Levees near the rivers Maas and Rhine risked collapse. Houses and commercial buildings were up to their roofs in water. More than 250,000 people had to move temporarily to safer areas and 10,000 livestock had to be evacuated to farms in dry parts of the country.

The national government rapidly installed an emergency team, which controlled the areas and the rise of the water. It took measures for a safe evacuation and for controlling the affected areas with empty houses, farms and enterprises. It was a huge operation that turned out well. Ultimately, the levees along the Maas and the Rhine were strong enough to hold back the water and did not collapse. However, in the province of Limburg, the area of the river Ijssel and in the greenhouse district of the Westland, the water did flood residential areas, market gardens and industrial zones. Fire departments from all over the country, the army and private companies did their utmost and worked hard during the months after the floods to pump away the water.

The power of the zoom lens

At the time, the national and international media paid a lot of attention to the situation. Cameras zoomed in, reporters inter-viewed mayors, farmers and residents of the affected areas, and talked to farmers looking after the evacuated livestock. The media came from all over the globe: from the neighbouring countries of Belgium, Germany and the UK, from the United States, Canada and even Japan. Newspapers, television and radio stations fed by their local correspondents and special camera and radio crews, flown to The Netherlands for the occa-sion, brought the news about the Dutch floods into the living rooms of many millions of households, from Stockholm to Cape

Town, from London to Tokyo, showing inundated areas, abandoned houses, farms and enterprises and people loading their belongings into vehicles and trailers.

This is when this crisis really began. The media attention paid to the floods 'helped' create an image of a whole country covered by water, ignoring the fact that only a relatively small area was inundated or was at risk. Most of The Netherlands, including the main tourist attractions, were accessible without any problem.

Tourists cancelling bookings

The telephones started ringing in the foreign offices of the Netherlands Board of Tourism (NBT), in Milan, New York, Los Angeles and Tokyo, to mention just a few. People intending to visit The Netherlands started asking themselves if the journey would still be worthwhile, or if the Low Countries could only be visited by boat. What about the tulip fields, the Rijksmuseum and Rembrandt's Night Watch, the Van Gogh Museum and its sunflowers, or the windmills at Kinderdijk? Could they be reached? What if the levees collapsed? The picture the foreign media painted was an alarming one, showing people escaping their homes and police forces patrolling ghost villages. Those watching the television news saw the country through the zoom lens of the camera, no more than that.

The effect was that people who did not know the country that well got the wrong picture. They started cancelling bookings, based only on the news and pictures they saw in the media. The information and press officers of the NBT's foreign offices did not appreciate the real situation in their home country, fed as they were by the same media. What they did understand was that tourists deciding to cancel their booking or not to book at all for trips to Amsterdam and the tourism highlights of The Netherlands were a real threat to the Dutch tourism industry. The country depends on tourism: 45,000 mainly small and medium-sized businesses employ 280,000 people in the industry. Tourist income at that time was worth €4 billion for the Dutch economy. Nowadays it is worth €8.3 billion.

The NBT offices abroad had to fight the power of the zoom lens with unequal resources, trying to tell customers the truth and to get across the real message about the floods. They needed objective information to present the right perspective. For instance: the flower fields bloom between March and May, whereas the floods were in January and February. Amsterdam was not affected, not even threatened, since it was too far from the affected areas. Rembrandt's Night Watch still had dry feet and Van Gogh's sunflowers had not been washed away. Trains were running, planes took off and landed at Amsterdam's Schiphol Airport, although it was four metres below sea level; and normal life in The Netherlands continued and it was more or less 'business as usual'.

An information network set in place

As soon as the communication department at the Dutch NBT headquarters became aware of the damage the media were creating with their take on the floods, a proactive communication strategy was designed, aimed at supplying the right information about the situation as quickly as possible to all its offices. A network of the most important information suppliers was set up and the communications department kept in close contact with them as long as necessary.

They asked for the weather forecast for the next few days from the national weather agency, KNMI. From Rijkswaterstaat, the governmental body for national infrastructure (roads and waterways), they requested forecasts for the amount of water flowing into Holland from France and Germany and the effect this could have on the threatened areas. They kept in touch with the national police force (KLPD) to get an accurate picture of traffic and the accessibility of roads and cities. The Dutch Railways (NS) informed them about the changes in their schedule and any train cancellations.

Each day – and at the start of the inundation, several times a day – colleagues in all 12 foreign offices of the NBT were updated, without exception. Detailed information was conveyed to them by phone and fax (e-mail not being current at that time), so they could inform their media contacts and the worried public around the world. The feedback from the offices was very positive, especially as this was the first time that communication on such an important topic had been designed and implemented. With this proactive strategy the damage to the image of The Netherlands as a safe holiday destination could be limited and corrected in a positive way.

Tourists appreciated the accurate information and, after a couple of weeks, bookings started to rise again. By the end of 1995 some 6.6 million foreign tourists had visited The

Netherlands, 6 per cent more than the year before. It would be too much to claim that this increase was due purely to the effective communication the NBT had set in place, but the prompt and accurate response to the questions of potential tourists did help to reassure them that the country was a safe holiday destination, worth visiting, and that the floods affected only a limited part of the country.

What were the lessons learnt?

The most important lesson is, start to communicate immediately, no matter how scant and incomplete your information might be. Fast information helps to counter any inaccurate or negative pictures the media publish from a disaster area and supports them in giving the right picture. Until 1995, the impact of (potential) natural disasters and the picture foreign media painted of them had never been considered in The Netherlands as a potential danger to the image foreign tourists can have of a holiday destination. Yet being aware of this possibility is important, as the Dutch economy depends heavily on incoming tourism.

The communication professionals at the NBT headquarters and in the offices abroad had never before cooperated so intensively on an issue in order to control the damage media attention can cause. The idea of sending objective information to the foreign offices of the NBT had a tremendously positive impact, first on the colleagues abroad, to whom the communications department in the NBT headquarters could add value, by supplying them with accurate and up-to-date information; second there was a positive impact on the image of The Netherlands in countries which are very important to Dutch tourism: Germany, Belgium, Great Britain, France, Italy, the United States and Japan.

Up-to-date information from several sources, coordinated and organized by the communications department of the NBT headquarters, helped to get the right message across and reassured the worried public. A side effect was that the press officers of the foreign offices could give their local press contacts the same information, contributing to downplaying the issue. In the years since the floods, the plans and information network set up have proven their value once again, during the foot and mouth crisis (2001) and the bird flu scare (2004).

Nowadays, the threatened levees have been strengthened and raised over a total of 148 kilometres. Another 147 kilometres of quays in cities along the rivers have been improved and fortified. The danger of flooding and breaching levees has been reduced to a minimum. The government has earmarked some thinly populated areas as land where excess water can be collected in times of emergency. What could have turned into a natural disaster has been limited mainly to financial damage.

Water control is in the genes of every Dutchman and the country is able to keep every inhabitant's feet dry. Still, the risk of flooding has become an issue again, following studies on climate change, global warming and the effects they could have on the sea level. Twenty-six per cent of The Netherlands is below sea level, and this is in the most populated areas; the lowest point of the country is 6.7 metres below sea level.

According to studies by the Dutch weather agency, KNMI, this century the sea level could rise by some 15–88 cm. Will we see cameras zoom in to flooded areas more frequently? And what will be the effect on the image of The Netherlands and the Dutch tourism sector when areas are flooded more often? The same questions might be asked of areas such as the Mississippi delta, the Nile delta, the lower parts of India, Bangladesh and the Indonesian Archipelago.

10 There is no substitute for media training

'No comment' just won't cut it any more

Nick Leighton (United Arab Emirates),
Steven Pellegrino (United States) and
Tony Shelton (United States)

Introduction

The goal of all crisis communication is protection of the organization's reputation – and profitability. Even an operational crisis response that is handled well can be overshadowed by a spokesperson who is hostile when interviewed by the media, is distant, or who just doesn't seem to have a sound grasp of the facts. In this chapter you'll find out why your spokespeople need media training, who should be trained, and how to train them.

When you have a crisis, the media are going to write stories about it with or without your assistance. It is in your best interests to participate in a story – especially a negative one – in order to have your position correctly represented. If you won't talk, the reporters will find someone who will – your competitors, local politicians or former employees. It's unlikely that they will put in a good word for you. For the media to report that 'No one from the company was available for comment' is to fuel speculation that you're hiding something – or worse. The best way to combat such a situation is to position yourself early on as the best source of information about your crisis. To do that, you will need to have spokespeople who have been trained in how to deal with the media under the most trying of circumstances.

Emmy Award-nominated NBC News reporter Dan Molina is now an executive media trainer with Shelton & Caudle in Houston, Texas. Molina says he has seen too many company spokespeople who are disorganized, frustrated that they are being thrust into the spotlight and openly angry at having to deal with the media in the first place. He says:

> Reporters can sense instantly when people are prepared and that they understand media attention is an inevitable component of a crisis. They put a human, caring face on the company and demonstrate to reporters and the public that the crisis, however severe, is in good hands.

A well-managed crisis response, communicated properly, can not only preserve your image and credibility; it can enhance it.

Who should we train?

After you've assembled your crisis communication team, one question inevitably comes to mind: 'Who should we train?' The short answer is: at least a handful of top management and a number of operational managers, as well as your professional communicators. A representative list might include the CEO, a trusted number two/top manager from the CEO's office, the COO, heads of various departments, public relations and marketing leaders, investor relations executives, security officials, and at least two managers from every facility or operating unit that's more than 20 miles from the main office.

Although not all of these individuals will need to be involved in every crisis, by having trained spokespeople in place you are likely to be able to locate an appropriate person and be able to have them at the site of the crisis quickly, if needed. Every one of them should be capable of instilling a level of confidence and calm, while conveying the message that the organization is in control of the situation – and not the other way around.

Another benefit of training a range of spokespeople is that you will be more easily able to match the level of the person to the level of the crisis. A PR person may be the appropriate spokesperson if you have a fire overnight and have to close a store. If people have been injured or someone has died, a member of top management may need to be the spokesperson, in order to show that the company takes the incident seriously and somebody in authority is making sure that what needs to be done is indeed taking place.

Who should do the training?

In selecting trainers for crisis communication, be sure to look for individuals who are experienced in this line of work. Agencies specializing in public relations only may not be experts in crisis training, even if they have assisted clients occasionally.

Here are some questions to ask:

- Who are some of your clients?
- Can you provide references?
- Do you provide crisis counsel, as well as training? (You want somebody who knows how to handle a crisis, not just talk about it.)
- Will you show me a sample training agenda?
- How many training sessions did you conduct last year?
- How long have you been in business?
- Will you be assigning senior trainers to my sessions or only your junior staff?
- What are your trainers' qualifications? Are any of them former journalists?

What you're looking for are experts who have long-term experience in crisis communication. *Caution*: just having been a journalist does not make a person a good media trainer.

Dan Molina of Shelton & Caudle says:

> What we've found by trying out some former reporters is that many of them just don't get how people should prepare to talk to reporters like themselves, let alone how to teach them to prepare messages for the media.

The bottom line is: search for experienced trainers who have worked with high-level executives in industries where crises are most common, such as healthcare, energy, the automotive sector, hospitality and government. Don't be too concerned if they don't have experience in your precise industry. There are two reasons for that: 1) crisis communication needs are the same no matter what the subject matter, and 2) if they're too familiar with your industry, they might be working with your competitors, too. A conflict of interest is not good for the trainer and certainly is not good for you.

Another recommendation: think *big*. Regardless of your company size or number of employees, there are advantages to working with a trainer who has experience with large clients and large-scale crisis communication. It is easier to grasp the magnitude and scope of a major, far-reaching or even global disaster, than it is a small one. And it's more valuable to role-play in a crisis that appears to be bigger than is typical for you or your company. It will challenge your spokespeople and give them confidence that they can deal with anything that comes their way.

Also, be very clear with deliverables. What will your people walk away with from this training? At a minimum, they should learn how to:

- interact and communicate effectively with the media during a crisis, and how to build and maintain trustworthy relationships;
- overcome anxiety when talking to the media;
- deliver a clear, concise and credible message to the media;
- handle unexpected or unfair questions;
- say they don't know or don't want to say (other than 'No comment');
- present information without appearing misinformed or overly emotional;
- maintain control, internally and externally;
- develop an initial response statement that can keep your spokesperson on track at a time of very high stress.

Deduct points if the trainer uses a PowerPoint presentation. That is likely to mean that you're getting one-size-fits-all instruction and a generalized crisis practice drill. What you want is a trainer who will not only customize a session tailored to your needs, but will also develop a crisis scenario for role-play that is both realistic and specific to your individual organization. If the trainer wants to add your participants to a general session with people from other organizations, keep looking. You can and should do better in your selection.

Other resources

While nothing can replace the experience of working face-to-face with an experienced trainer, there are other good resources. The internet brings virtual crisis management training to your fingertips 24 hours a day, seven days a week. Industry organizations or affiliations that specialize in your line of business often have training seminars, webcasts or videos that can be purchased for in-company training. For example, the American Hotel & Lodging Association offers its resources and training programmes to hotels across the country. Likewise, the National Restaurant Association can be a useful source of information when real-life emergencies occur.

Who are the media?

The training should include at least a brief discussion of the various types of reporters and media, as well as their particular needs and pressures. Understanding the different journalists and editors will allow you to meet their needs:

- *Staff journalists*: are idealistic, usually inexperienced, frequently under pressure and underpaid. They can become aware of the power of their position and can be difficult.
- *Freelance journalists*: often specialist professionals, in for the long haul. Self-employed, they want to build long-term relationships and are looking for economical ways of working.
- *News journalists*: working on tighter deadlines, will want shorter quotes and opinions. They will be hard to reach and you need to be very concise with them.
- *Features journalists*: longer deadlines and more analytical.
- *Trade journalists*: more likely to know your industry – and your secrets. Their readers are also more literate, so the language and acronyms used are more industry-specific than general.

Timing – internet/daily/weekly/monthly

Be aware that all these different journalists are working to different deadlines and have different priorities. You should be aware of the publishing deadline, too. For example, a monthly industry title that comes out on the first of July may 'close' the issue on 22 June to allow time for design, printing and distribution.

In the end, all journalists are looking for the same things. They all want stories, ideas, information, anecdotes – and most of all they want controversy. Your crisis will be fitted into the category of controversy if at all possible. Was someone negligent? Whose fault was it? How could you allow something like this to happen? But in hurricanes and floods and other natural disasters, there is no one to blame, right? Wrong. Why didn't somebody give us better information sooner? Why didn't somebody help us? Thus the controversial part of the story is born.

Developing the crisis message

The mantra of developing a crisis message is:

anticipate – prepare – rehearse.

When it comes to a crisis, you can't expect journalists to ask you the 'right' question that allows you to get your messages across – they won't! You have to create opportunities. But first you have to know what you're going to say. You have to develop, work out and learn the message that you want to get across and, with luck, it will be what appears on the page or screen.

The message you want to send out to the journalists has to be carefully planned and developed. There cannot be anything casual or impromptu about it. It has to be thought through, so that the journalists get all the information they need and all the information you want them to have, in a positive, straightforward way. Learning how to develop the crisis message should be an integral part of media training involving crisis communication. Ideally, your crisis message will have:

- Credibility – so that the journalist has confidence in the message and belief in you.
- Appropriate context – for the journalist and programme or publication.
- Right content – that is appropriate for the viewer, listener or reader.
- Clarity – so that the message is unequivocal.
- Simplicity – so that the message will not be misinterpreted and will be reported consistently.

The easiest way to keep yourself on track is to prepare a brief, written 'holding' or response statement, just as soon as you can. You can read it to reporters over the phone and deliver it in person before the cameras. At the same time, others can be using the same written statement to respond to enquiries from other reporters and to inform other important stakeholder groups, such as employees and relevant officials.

Having a written statement that contains most of the information that you, 1) have, and 2) feel comfortable releasing, serves another purpose, too. It keeps you from having to repeatedly respond to reporters' questions with variations of 'I don't know.' Even though you're not expected to have all the answers right away, such an episode can kill your confidence as it does away with your credibility.

However, if the crisis continues for a while or escalates – for example, if injured employees later die – you will need to do a media update. At that point, you can start out with a prepared statement but you, or your executive, must be ready to take questions.

Know the rules of the game

Here are some general rules, all of which should be delivered to participants in a media training session.

General rules of communication in a crisis

Preparation

- Have your messages well prepared and rehearsed with key note cards, but no long pages of information that you can trip over.
- Memorize your messages – the key words, not entire sentences.
- Learn the facts – 100 per cent correct and accurate. Guessing is not allowed.

Introductions

- Dealing with reporters is not a social gathering and there is no time for longwinded introductions. Introduce yourself and then get to the point.

How you speak

- The shorter your sentence, the more powerful it will be. Think 'sound bite'.
- Be as clear and concise as possible.
- Use emotional language only in expressing your concern for people affected by the incident.
- Imagine your listener has the comprehension of a 12 year-old and communicate at that level.

- Start at the beginning, not with the conclusion; lead the listener.
- Don't lie or mislead – ever.
- You don't have to include everything; just keep to the question and on message.
- Avoid jargon and industry-specific terms or acronyms unless you define them clearly.
- Numbers can help give you credibility, but use only a few and keep them rounded for simplicity.

Being media friendly

- If journalists are making notes do not speak too fast, and repeat key words or phrases.
- If a journalist offends you, tell the person so politely, but do not lose your temper. (That could become the story.)
- You can repeat a question that is asked of you, to ensure that you are answering what the journalist asks.

The end

- It is your option when to end the interview. (Don't forget to do that when you're practising in media training, as well.)

Classic responses

Here are some classic responses to awkward questions:

- I'm very glad you asked me that...
- That's a very important question, but even more important is...
- Before I answer that question, I think I should say that...
- That's a very good question, and I will answer it in a minute, but before I do...
- I think what you meant by that question is...
- I don't have the exact details, but what I can say is...

Don't be afraid to contradict or correct:

- You might say that, but my experience is...
- No, that is not true. The truth is...
- I think you are wrong. In my view...
- Please let me finish...

Don't be afraid to say you don't know. Also, be honest – but you don't have to tell the whole truth (everything you know).

Conducting the training

Training includes two important aspects – the learning or skill-building and the practising. The more you practise, the better you'll be at crisis communication.

Our combined years of conducting general and crisis communication training sessions have taught us that the following elements are essential to successful training.

Training concept 1 – engage the participants from the time they arrive until they depart

Conduct a short interview with each person as they arrive. The premise of the interview can be simply to gather information about their company and their job, with maybe a company-specific 'zinger' included to get their attention.

As you build skills – messaging, how to handle tough questions – conduct additional practice before you transition into the crisis drill.

Training concept 2 – put them on camera

Although participants dread it, training evaluations show they nearly all say it was the most useful tool of the day. Video playback is a fantastic way for spokespeople to really see how they perform. This is particularly useful for spokespeople who need to see their own speaking peculiarities and learn how to control them. Playback is also a great time to help them focus on the things they are doing well to help build their confidence, as well as to provide tips on how to improve.

Training concept 3 – include actual journalists as interviewers

We actually disagree about the advisability of using journalists who are currently working in news. One of us is more comfortable using reporters, especially from TV, who are not currently working as journalists. In any event, their presence heightens the realism of the experience for the participants, and the journalists can provide real-life experiences with companies that have handled their crisis communications well and some that have not.

Training concept 4 – use pre-written scenarios

Design them to be specific and realistic for the individual client. The degree of complexity is up to you. For example, the premise could be as simple as: 'Your company headquarters has gone up in flames. Here's a reporter who wants to ask you about it.'

You could then provide written updates to the interviewees, with more specifics included in each round. The interviewees would have the task of deciding which of the new details should be released and then deliver them as messages in the next round.

The variations and embellishments to this basic approach are nearly endless. You can distribute a fake internet 'news update' or have staff members call into the training room pretending to be reporters, customers, or outraged neighbours. We very often go so far as to visit a client facility to record fake TV news reports to be used in the drill.

Conclusion

The dual keys to successful crisis media training are: 1) preparation, and 2) practice. In fact, those are the same keys to a successful crisis communication. Please keep them in mind the next time your organization is facing a crisis.

When media training, it is important to ensure the right team is trained so there is full coverage should a crisis occur. While there are resources available online and in print format, you will probably look to an experienced PR agency for outside assistance. In this chapter we looked at how to choose the right agency with the right experience for your organization. We also looked at exactly what should be taught in the training – who the press are, how to deal with the press and how to deal with those difficult questions. We also looked at the advantages of using learning tools such as video, professional journalists and pre-prepared scenarios during your training sessions.

11 How senior management can make the crisis worse

Crisis plans are likely to fail without the full participation of the board

Stuart Hyslop (United Kingdom)

Introduction

The aim of this chapter is to highlight the crucial need for any crisis plan to have buy-in at the highest level of your company or organization. Without the total support and full participation of the board, any crisis plan is likely to fail. Sadly, too few organizations accept this and even fewer practise it.

How it can all go wrong

You have a crisis team trained, you have excellent facilities and equipment in place and you are delighted with the spokesperson who will confidently defend the reputation of your company. Nothing, you think, has been left to chance. Wrong.

Unless the top management in your company or organization have also been trained in how they should respond in a crisis, there is a strong likelihood that things will go wrong. The managing director (or chief executive officer) and his or her fellow executive directors must also be trained, although not in the same way as the rest of the team. Their role is very different, but they need to understand this. The worst thing that can happen is for them – and for everyone else – to discover this during a full-blown crisis.

Getting senior people to accept they need training is not always easy. Some will refuse to take part because they simply don't believe anything will ever happen that is sufficiently serious for them to become involved; others because they believe it is beneath them; some because they are terrified of being 'exposed' as ill-equipped with the necessary skills; and there will be those who are simply too busy (or make damn sure they appear to be).

These are understandable defence mechanisms. Successful executives would be less than human if they did not have more than the average measure of intellectual arrogance, or suffer from the Edward de Bono 'intelligence trap', whereby bright people habitually defend their inherently superior opinions against all-comers.

Managing to make it worse

Here are some quick examples of what I mean.

The director of communications at a major UK utility who claimed he had been involved in loads of crisis. He had all the T-shirts and didn't need any training. He was torn to pieces in his first live television interview and never recovered.

Another director of communications at a UK utility who made sure she was always away on important business whenever we turned up to train the senior team. Needless to say she had still not completed one coherent press release and was in tears when we shut down the subsequent 'live' exercise.

Then there were the representatives of all the government departments of a European state who admitted they doubted they would be able to get quick agreement on a joint press statement because they found it difficult sharing such information for 'political' reasons. The exercise was a disaster but that didn't prevent the minister in charge from turning up and announcing to the expectant media that it had been a great success.

There was a managing director of a huge conglomerate in the Far East who was cocooned by his over-respectful staff and PR team. We trained them but were never able to get near him. Consequently he floundered and appeared out of touch and distinctly 'off-message' at a press conference during a crisis. He left the company shortly afterwards.

According to the *Harvard Business Review,* 'most companies do an inadequate job of managing their reputations in general and the risks to their reputations in particular'. Any CEO or board should be aware of the vital need for crisis training. Research, for instance that conducted by Oxford Metrica, underlines that the fortunes of a company or organization during and following a corporate crisis, for better or – more commonly – for worse, depend upon the perceived competence of the board in dealing with it. Further research has shown that it can take years for a company's share price to recover fully after a crisis if it is believed that it was handled badly.

Getting it right

The textbook example of how to respond to a crisis was given by Sir Michael Bishop, British Midland's chairman, in 1989 after one of his aircraft crashed near the M1 motorway in the Midlands, killing 47 people and injuring 74.

Bishop went immediately to the scene, took responsibility and personally dealt with the media in an open and honest manner. He was reassuring and authoritative, so much so that the crash became known as the Kegworth (where the plane crashed) rather than British Midland, disaster.

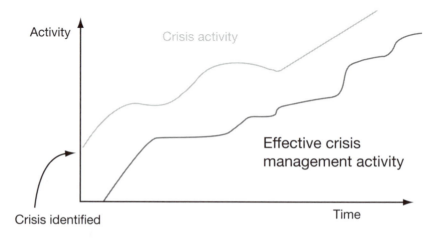

Figure 11.1 Crisis that controls you

By acting so decisively Bishop revealed an impressive understanding of how to lead during a crisis and when under intense media scrutiny. He was always available, open, sympathetic and helpful. Despite the enormity of the disaster (caused by mechanical failure and pilot error), the public did not lose their trust in British Midland.

Contrast that with the damage done to turkey farmer Bernard Matthews, one of the UK food industry's best known brands. It suffered an outbreak of the bird flu virus H5N1 at a turkey farm in Norfolk in early 2007. Despite reassurances, journalists kept revealing information that the company should have been releasing.

Mr Matthews did not adopt the Sir Michael Bishop approach. Sales slumped due to a loss of public confidence – particularly after the source of the virus was revealed to be turkey meat imported from a sister factory in Hungary. This story is more likely to become a textbook study for all the wrong reasons.

As Gary Davies, Manchester Business School's Professor of Corporate Reputation, says (contrary to the advice you will get from many corporate lawyers) the best way to protect and perhaps save your business's shaky reputation in a crisis is to: 'get the boss out front, apologize for your mistakes and take the hit'.

Companies quoted on the London Stock Exchange are now obliged to have strong risk management strategies in place and to report these to shareholders. A common approach is to generate a risk register and to develop business continuity, communication and security plans. Such plans are, however, often not united under effective board own-

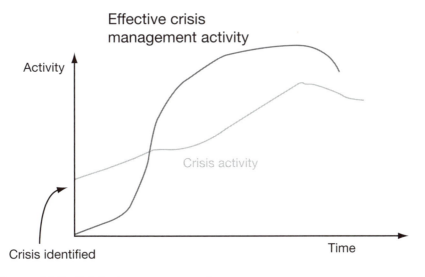

Figure 11.2 Crisis that you control

ership. Moreover, in the absence of corporate crisis experience, many boards assume that their knowledge and experience will enable them to deal with a crisis, when it comes, as a high-level, high-speed mutation of routine business.

A consequence is that often corporate crisis arrangements lack a top-level perspective. They are not realistically tested at top level or rehearsed regularly. Proverbially, there is an understandable reluctance to confront an issue that may never happen. There is, however, collateral evidence that the worst time to learn how to manage a crisis is during the crisis itself.

Veterans of serious corporate crises emphasize that there comes a moment of judgement when the board itself, in harmony with the executive committee (if applicable), must reconfigure quickly to face and resolve the precipitative demands of wild pressures that impinge suddenly from all directions. There are well-tried guidelines for reorganizing top management very quickly in the face of impending corporate mayhem that can overcome many of the predictable and paralysing effects of the onslaught, and enhance greatly a company's ability to achieve rational and effective decisions and generally to perform under pressure.

How to demonstrate leadership

It is necessary to avoid two extremes of difficulty. One is the impulse to make decisions quickly that then prove wrong but difficult to unravel. The other is to defer essential decisions repeatedly whilst seeking clarification of a galloping situation.

'Leadership in crisis,' says Jeremy Larken, of Octo, which my own company partners, 'requires those in charge to be willing to devote the highest initial priority to determining what is actually going on.' This may involve extracting the nuggets from an avalanche of information, or to divine the reality from a dearth of hard facts. In both cases, it may be a question of reading the correct weak signals from amidst the 'noise'.

Plainly it involves taking responsibility, but the means by which this responsibility is exercised and delegation assigned is likely to be crucial. Here's Larken's favourite quote on responsibility, which always wins rueful acknowledgement and with which private sector executives are perhaps more comfortable than some public sector colleagues amidst the complexities of government organization and ministerial accountability:

Responsibility is a unique concept: it can only reside and inhere in a single individual. You may share it with others, but your portion is not diminished. You may delegate it, but it is still with you. Even if you do not recognize it or admit its presence, you cannot escape it. If responsibility is rightfully yours, no evasion, or ignorance, or passing the blame can shift the burden to someone else. Unless you can point your finger at the man who is responsible when something goes wrong, then you have never had anyone really responsible. (Admiral Hyman G Rickover, 1961, Joint Committee on Atomic Energy, Radiation Safety and Regulation, Washington)

One notable trait to be found in some CEOs is 'an excessive appetite for being "in the hot seat"', which means they take all the decisions themselves and don't delegate. Larken says:

Some feel obliged to make lots of big decisions quickly and with inadequate information; subsequently there is cause to repent but their actions cannot readily be unravelled. At the other end of the spectrum, some may wait until the situation becomes clearer and end up making no decision at all.

Our aim is to help prepare the executive to navigate the middle way between these two extremes. It's also to instil a capacity to recognize that over-centralization beyond the really important big decisions can prove fatally inefficient in fast-moving situations when one casualty is likely to be efficient communications.

A typical problem experienced by, for example, national groups of large multinationals in a local crisis – for instance a national terrorist situation such as many UK companies and organizations have faced in recent times – is head office dictating detailed actions and policies from afar with a poor understanding of the situation 'on the ground'. Larken cites the example of a large US company that flew in a senior executive to take charge of its UK group of companies in just these circumstances. 'He took charge in a loud and aggressive way and quickly succeeded in alienating everyone. It makes life extremely difficult in terms of trying to generate effective leadership and coherent direction.'

On a somewhat different note, Larken recalls the time when a large UK defence organization had a change at the top to a very dominant CEO who summarily cancelled a crucial crisis training exercise because he was unnerved by the realities that he feared would emerge. It was never re-scheduled. 'It's a form of institutional constipation and can be costly – not just in financial terms.'

Avoidance is endemic

These problems are not restricted to the private sector. In my experience senior civil servants tend to have a well-developed antipathy to the prospect of being in the hot seat. I have witnessed numerous occasions when individuals have chosen to duck below the parapet by referring what should be personal decisions to committees.

This form of avoidance is endemic everywhere. You see it in government, local authorities and other civic bodies: strenuous efforts to avoid accountability. There's simply little or no culture of accepting responsibility. And it's not just prevalent in the UK: it's found in most countries. Civil servants do not see themselves as deliverers. They will go to great lengths to advise their minister and guard their ministry. But to be in the firing line, to carry the can if things go wrong – no chance. Without accountability going down the line you can't run anything.

Returning to how a board should structure crisis preparedness. Unfortunately, all too often the responsible board member delegates too completely to a lead department – usually public relations, security, risk management or business continuity. Larken comments:

> The problem with this is that you tend to end up with a parochial crisis plan prepared very much from that department's point of view. Usually it is a PR or media plan which is somewhat one-dimensional and naïve. It's not holistic and is correspondingly fragile.
>
> You badly need a holistic plan because under extreme pressure in a crisis the board has got to start operating in a very different way to what it does normally. It's not ordinary business speeded up. It's liable to be a matter of totally unexpected and unfamiliar problems and issues flying at the board from all directions. If you try and treat it as ordinary business speeded up you will run into the quicksand very fast.
>
> The board needs to recognize this is a real issue and should reconfigure its structure to deal with it. But persuading a board to do this or bringing it to its attention and getting them to treat it seriously is quite an art form. Yet to do so in the midst of crisis is exceedingly difficult – yet another factor obscuring reality in the worst of circumstances.

Some boards understand this. Crisis is bound to be a feature of life, for instance, for hydrocarbon 'majors', and all of them take their crisis management arrangements very seriously. There are, however, a surprising number of prestigious companies where the board does not have an effective and tested structure in place to deal with a major corporate incident. Examples are plans that comprise a not very coherent amalgam of corporate communications and business continuity.

Of course the board will consist of bright and able people who will expect to be able to sit down and sort out whatever problems arise, but they may find that in the event they are overwhelmed. They simply won't be prepared for the huge complexities and speed of events that engulf them; nor will the organization be able to rapidly adapt to provide them with the crucial services they need. Larken says:

> Unless you really do think through crisis management and have a real plan which involves the board and is tested and practised, crisis will prove a traumatic experience and your business is likely to be seriously damaged.
>
> Most crises damage a business in some way but we're talking here about the difference between reducing the impact from say 80 per cent to more like 30 per cent probability. That's a huge impact on your resilience.

The danger signs

What are the danger signs we should all be alerted to when assessing the likelihood of a company or organization hitting the headlines for all the wrong reasons? There are the obvious ones such as rampant corporate greed – ridiculously expensive corporate headquarters, inflated salaries and perks and a semi-detached connection with the real world. Then there's the all too familiar 'not invented here' syndrome where advice and best practice from outside the comfortable corporate cocoon is eschewed in favour of so-called home-grown expertise.

Helen Shannon of Octo reports a particularly alarming trend. She points out that businesses know very well what they are spending on loss prevention. But it is much more difficult to quantify the benefits of this crucial 'insurance policy'. Cutting back on loss prevention, for example on scheduled maintenance, is a tempting target for economies.

But at what point, a point by nature imprecise, does this cease to be safe? Railtrack and BP are two UK companies that would appear to have judged this poorly, precipitating crises and leading arguably to the demise of Railtrack and serious current damage to BP.

All boards can only function as well as the quality of the support they receive. A cadre of senior managers has also got to understand the crisis arrangements ready to support the board or the executive group handling the crisis on the board's behalf. This means they too must be well trained and should take part in high-quality exercises.

There is a simple law here that works on the basis that senior people will rapidly absorb the essential lessons and will provide the kind of advice you need with far less training than is required for more junior people. The more junior the people you take on to support the board the more you have to train them.

There must be board ownership. A board member must be genuinely responsible for all this and he or she must play a hands-on role in the creation and testing of a comprehensive crisis plan. Everyone should be consulted and drawn in to make sure the plan is harmonized. It must be holistic.

It must also be practised well and tested. Once the system is established and proven, a substantial annual exercise should be sufficient – provided the CEO and his or her executive crisis team are genuinely involved. It won't work if it's not done properly, with performances measured against sensible criteria.

Conclusion

Dealing with a crisis from a leader's perspective

The challenges posed by a crisis will affect people in different and perhaps unpredictable ways. What is certain is that the pressures upon individuals will be immense. The leadership demands imposed upon all senior people involved will probably be substantially different and more searching than those of routine high-level business. Myriad aggravations, from 'groupthink' to the inroads of exhaustion, will all be encountered.

Collateral benefits of crisis preparation

Executives and managers who have addressed crisis management in a systematic way report an interesting and very positive side-effect. This is that their day-to-day management skills, decisions, objectivity and completion of tasks to programme are enhanced.

Getting to grips

The aim therefore is to identify, grip and control a crisis quickly and decisively. The prime areas to address are:

- strategic assessment tools, including crisis risk assessment;
- crisis organization;
- managing information in a crisis;
- links with key stakeholders.

Managing reputation

Reputation must of course be based on substance. Presentation with integrity is therefore a vital function. This by no means demands complete openness, warts and all, but adherence to core values and cognisance of some basic human reactions. The question of when to present key information opens the dilemma between winning hearts and minds, and waiting for greater accuracy. The importance of keeping one's own people informed cannot be over-emphasized.

12 Judgement days

How a company handles a legal dispute can salvage or spoil its reputation

Kathryn Tunheim (United States)

Introduction

A company's reputation is shaped over many years by myriad factors. One of the chief influencers of public perception of an organization is how that organization reacts in a crisis. Decisions made about how to navigate through a challenging situation – in this case, a disaster resulting in serious injury and a subsequent legal dispute – can maintain, destroy or even bolster a company's reputation.

Very frequently, organizations find themselves needing to straddle reputation management efforts in more than one forum: the court of public opinion and the legal courtroom itself. Ensuring optimal results in both forums can be extraordinarily challenging. Given the likely stakes and the technical expertise required to navigate the legal system, these disputes put particular pressure on the abilities of communication professionals, lawyers and top executives to work together effectively.

Operating in the court of public opinion and in the legal system simultaneously requires acceptance of some basic ground rules:

- As in any dispute, it is important to understand the multiple interests and sensitivities of the players in conflict.
- It is critical that the reputation management team understand the varying 'rules of engagement' in each of the forums involved: rules

of the legal system; rules of journalism; rules of corporate decision making when facing litigation (governance role, for example).

- There is a need to articulate key messages in the terms and the tones that are appropriate for each forum: the language of litigation doesn't play well in the media – and judges don't want to see their cases 'tried in the press'.
- Finally, each of the forums puts unique constraints on the communication process – and so has consequences for the effectiveness of messaging overall.

Case study

Situation summary

A United States-based petroleum company operated a large refinery in a Midwestern suburban community, and had invested years in developing trusted relationships with neighbourhood groups and public safety officials. On a spring day in 1997, an explosion in a sewer line ignited a massive fire; five employees were injured, one of them severely enough to later certify him as permanently and fully disabled. Fire crews from numerous adjacent communities were involved in bringing the fire under control; the subsequent regulatory review cited five safety violations as a result of the investigation after the incident.

Even as the company worked diligently in the succeeding months and years to rebuild the trust of neighbours, public officials and employees about the safety and integrity of its operations, litigation associated with the injuries to the employees was making its way through the federal legal system. Because US labour laws limited the potential for an injured employee to pursue awards for damages beyond the relevant insurance coverage, the most seriously injured employee encouraged the government to investigate the need for additional safety measures at the plant. After extensive investigation by the US attorney's office, the company was charged with violation of the Clear Air Act, and with making false statements to state regulators about the safety of its sewer system.

Prior to initiation of a court trial five years later, which would have brought back dramatic and emotional coverage about the incident for the company and the affected employees, the company settled its legal issues with the US government, the injured employees and the public safety officials in their community. It paid more than US

$7 million in fines and restitution – more than half of that sum going to the most severely injured individual. In addition, it agreed to spend more than US $4 million on improvements to the plant's sewer system, and paid significant amounts to the communities whose fire departments fought the blaze years earlier.

Key considerations and risks

The allegations being made by the federal government against the company and its officials were very serious – any attempt to minimize the seriousness of the situation would have alienated both the plant employees and the public officials who had conducted the investigation into what went wrong. At the same time, the plant was running a full production schedule and needed to project the confidence that all systems and operating functions were under control – any problems that might have existed had been fully resolved.

There had been a change in the ownership of the plant in the years between the incident and the settlement: the original owner had become a joint venture partner with another petroleum company. While some of the management personnel were the same, the decision-making process for both the legal settlement and the public relations strategy had to be altered slightly, to respect the changed ownership. There had been subsequent incidents at the plant – none as significant, none resulting in human injuries – but still, adverse publicity had impacted the general public's sense of confidence in the trustworthiness of the company's pronouncements about safety.

While the legal charges were being levied against the company, it was individual executives from the company who needed to appear in court and in news broadcasts, in order for both the legal courtroom and the 'court of public opinion' to conclude that the company was accepting its responsibilities. It was not good enough to talk through the lawyers.

Essential programme elements

The actual settlement of legal claims was prepared to meet the terms and requirements of the federal court. Guilty pleas were entered on two misdemeanour counts; a deferred prosecution agreement related to other charges was documented; and an executive of the company appeared in court to enter the pleas.

Media materials were prepared for use in journalists' coverage of the settlement: individual managers were quoted as accepting responsibility on behalf of the company for the mistakes made, and for the tragic consequences for employees. The managers expressed deep regret for the failure of the company to meet its own standards.

Editorial backgrounders were prepared and distributed to explicitly lay out the various elements of the settlement – in language that consumers could understand. Editorial backgrounders were also prepared to explain the significant change in the company's overall approach to safety in the years since the incident, including its decision to serve as a national model for acceptance of an entirely new level of industry guidelines, built on a worldwide compliance network.

An advertisement was prepared and placed, to be published on the day after the settlement was accepted by the US district judge. It apologized to the community in general for the incident and its tragic consequences – and again, outlined the changed commitments of the company in the years since the incident.

Spokesperson training was conducted for the managers tasked with representing the company, both in the courtroom (which would be filled with media), and in the subsequent media conference. Other managers were prepared to handle all employee communications onsite at the refinery. A speaking packet was prepared for use by company managers in the subsequent weeks, to share the story effectively with community, business and public safety groups, as the company began the long process of rebuilding its trust relationship with employees and neighbours.

Results and lessons learnt

Media coverage of the settlement was almost as extensive as the dramatic coverage of the fire itself years earlier. Coverage included effective representation of the company by its managers: they were articulate, empathetic and sincere. Government lawyers were measured in their comments, and coverage overall was balanced and unemotional.

Employee meetings went well: more important than the messages delivered were the messengers themselves. It mattered a lot to employees that the company management took responsibility and committed to a higher standard of safety moving forward.

The strategy to coordinate communication, but to provide completely customized materials to the two 'courts' worked well.

> Media and the public got what they needed and seemed to understand and accept what was offered. The legal system was well-served and allowed to maintain the dignity of its protocols and practices – there was no 'media circus' or manipulation of what needed to be a very deliberate and precise process of sorting out and accepting responsibilities and consequences.

Operating simultaneously in the legal system and in the court of public opinion requires careful orchestration, and should be built on solid understanding of the 'rules of engagement' in each environment. There will be unavoidable constraints going back and forth – the reputation management team must navigate through them.

The language of public discourse is not the same as the language of the legal system. Legalistic jargon gets in the way of creating understanding or empathy when it finds its way into a company's public statements. Conversely, judicial officials are not amused when they find themselves the setting for a media feeding-frenzy. Respecting the needs of each environment is critical.

In general, the time involved to move a matter through the legal system will far outstretch the media (or the public) attention span. As a result, major milestones in a legal dispute carry the risk of creating visibility 'bounces' that are often out of line with their legal significance, simply because they reintroduce the original story of the conflict. In the case above, a five year-old incident is replayed in significant detail upon news of its legal settlement, and duplicates the reputational risk that the company faced at the time of the original event. The communication challenge, then, is to optimize the potential for balancing the story in a way that was impossible at the time of the incident, in order to rebuild the reputation that was tarnished.

Conclusion

Companies working their way through litigation must act responsibly, honestly and respectfully. Those injured by a company's actions – even if those actions are completely unintentional – must be considered first and foremost. A company must do the right thing by telling its side of the story in a forthright manner (including taking responsibility, if appropriate), compensating fairly, and showing in a tangible way how it will rectify a bad situation. Only by taking the high road can a company hope to salvage a damaged reputation.

13 Environmental crisis communications

Learning from the lessons of the past to maintain corporate and brand value

Robert J Oltmanns (United States)

Introduction

Environmental communication is not just for manufacturers anymore. Nor is it something limited to the nuclear power industry, petrochemicals or hazardous waste incineration. Today, environmental stewardship is a cornerstone of virtually every business or enterprise. Understanding and embracing the new era of environmental awareness and consciousness in every corner of the global economy will help add value to a corporation's brand, its reputation, and its bottom line.

Environmental communication was born out of necessity in the wake of a series of industrial disasters that came on the heels of heightened public awareness and concern for the environment. The movement that began with Rachel Carson's seminal book, *Silent Spring* and was followed by a raising of global consciousness during the first Earth Day, was eventually crystallized in the minds of people around the world with the outcry over nuclear power in the 1970s.

Prior to that time, environmental compliance was neither a priority nor a common business practice. Government environmental oversight and regulation barely existed prior to 1970 when the US Environmental Protection Agency was first created. At that time, fines were low and easy to pay, and were regarded as little more than a nuisance in industrial management. But a series of historic events captured the attention of the world and helped usher in a new era of environmental stewardship in business, government, and society:

- *Amoco Cadiz* oil supertanker accident, Brittany, France, 16 March 1978.
- Discovery of Hooker Chemical Company dumpsite at Love Canal, Niagara Falls, New York, February 1979.
- Accident at the Three Mile Island Nuclear Power Station, Middletown, Pennsylvania, 28 March 1979.
- Accident at Union Carbide India, Bhopal, India, 3 December 1984.
- *Exxon Valdez* oil supertanker accident, Prince William Sound, Alaska, 24 March 1989.

These environmental crises forever changed the face of industrial management and set in motion a global revolution of environmental consciousness that cut across all geopolitical and socioeconomic boundaries. Where polluted air once meant prosperity and progress, it now represented a global health hazard that would cripple future generations. For the first time, science and the conventional wisdom concluded that the earth was a finite and delicate ecosystem that could not withstand increasing levels of pollution.

That period of environmental consciousness triggered a global turning point – first in the United States and Europe and later in parts of Asia. In just a 15-year period between the early 1970s and late 1980s, a new era of environmental awareness, advocacy and regulation was born and with it, a new generation of environmentally-conscious consumers, voters, investors and neighbours. As the age of innocence transitioned to the post-industrial economy, the world's common vocabulary suddenly included words that previously were reserved for the scientific community: carcinogens, PCBs, plutonium, CFCs, ozone, dioxin, mercury and others. Public outrage over environmental contamination brought about by industrial pollution turned the spotlight on manufacturing practices, and corporations around the world were placed in a position of having to explain themselves for the first time in history.

The business world was slow to respond and corporations earned the reputation of being an enemy of the environment. Forced into compliance by government regulation, pressured to adopt more environmentally safe operations by NGOs, and accused by the news media of 'midnight dumping' and other crimes against the environment, big business was among the last to willingly embrace the global environmental movement.

However, after the *Exxon Valdez* accident in 1989, a new vision of environmental stewardship in business emerged with such doctrines as the 'Valdez Principles' and the American Chemistry Council's 'Responsible Care'™ programme, among others. These management models paved the way for business, government and environmental organizations to work in partnership to reduce the environmental impact of manufacturing around the world.

Today, environmental stewardship is far more commonplace in industry, and not just in manufacturing industries, but in the service sector, retail, entertainment, food and beverage, travel and tourism, transport and virtually every aspect of the global economy. Yet still, businesses and organizations whose operations hold the potential for environmental impact are vulnerable to crisis situations. Accidents still do happen. Human error, acts of God, terrorism, weather or geologic events, and other calamities, when they occur near hazardous materials, can still prove disastrous for the environment, wildlife and human health.

Fortunately, the experience and lessons learnt from past environmental crises have provided a valuable roadmap for creating a culture of environmental stewardship and then effectively surviving an environmental crisis. These lessons are the foundation of environmental management in any business or industry, and are an essential set of strategies for running an enterprise and surviving crises in this new era of environmental consciousness.

Laying the groundwork: creating a culture of environmental stewardship

Effective environmental crisis communication cannot occur in a vacuum. It needs to be a logical extension of an enterprise-wide culture of environmental management and stewardship that factor into the organization's overall corporate reputation and brand identity. An organization that doesn't discover environmental stewardship until it is faced with a crisis will risk being perceived as disingenuous and artificial in its management of the crisis. Environmental stewardship as a foundation of corporate culture will not only guide organizational decision making in times of crisis: it will help maintain and add value to the corporate brand. Such principles of environmental stewardship include the following.

Demonstrating environmental leadership

The best strategy for earning a reputation as a responsible steward of the environment is to actually be one. That doesn't simply mean doing an occasional good deed, because environmental organizations will easily recognize that as 'greenmail' or 'greenwash'. Rather, demonstrating environmental leadership means making a serious and legitimate commitment to development and adhering to sound environmental management practices in all aspects of your business, particularly those that could have the greatest impact on the environment. Often this comes at a significant financial investment. But the experience of industry leaders has been that such environmental management practices are purely good business and, more to the point, they are simply the way that business is conducted in this era of increased environmental awareness.

Establishing credible environmental partnerships

'No man is an island' and no business can exist as an island, particularly one that can reasonably be expected to be accountable for its impact on the environment.

Good business practice dictates that partnerships with environmental organizations be cultivated and maintained by taking an active role in the programmes and political agenda of these organizations. The mission of most NGOs is to make an impact and demonstrating productive partnerships with the private sector shows to foundation and government funding sources that their financial support is making a difference. Such partnerships will serve you well in times of crisis, when community support is needed and the approval of the environmental community becomes a much-needed vote of confidence that helps your organization through the pressure and scrutiny of an environmental challenge.

Establishing productive communication relationships

When a crisis occurs, it will be too late to begin developing relationships with your local media, government officials, civic leaders, the business community and others. The time to begin building and cultivating those relationships is now, without the heat and pressure of a crisis looming over your organization.

Make sure that your operations are known and understood – if only on a rudimentary level – by those in your community. Fear and panic will ensue during a crisis if your facility is the subject of mystery and ignorance, a burden that you will have to bear if you fail to take the mystery out of your operations and enlighten your neighbours, their elected leaders and the local media.

Publishing your environmental values and making sure you live up to them

Most companies now publish – either in print or online – an environmental annual report, environmental mission statement, stewardship plan, or similar document that outlines the manner in which the environment fits into the company's overall corporate social responsibility strategy and business plan.

By articulating your organization's commitment to sound environmental management practices, you instantly send a message that the environment is an important dimension of your business. You take this responsibility seriously enough to put it in writing for all the world to see, including customers, employees, investors, lenders, government leaders, the media and the community. Living up to the standards you define will give you the reputation and credibility you need in times of crisis.

Understanding the impact and pitfalls of risk communication

People who live in close proximity to industrial facilities are often mindful, if not resentful, of the fact that they live with risk every day. When the discipline of environmental communication first came of age, meaningless comparisons were forced upon employees and neighbours of industrial facilities in an attempt to trivialize the relative risk in favour of the facility.

'There's only a one in million chance that anyone could get cancer from exposure to anything at this facility,' said many in industry. 'That's the same as one drop of gasoline in a tank full of gas.' Comparisons like this were seen as a great way to communicate relative risk in the nuclear power, petrochemical, hazardous waste and other industries for many years.

But industry's zeal to equate scientific probability with everyday experiences, while well-intentioned, ultimately proved to be ineffective. A one in a million risk might seem to be a practical impossibility, but what if that one in a million cancer risk was my child or me? Suddenly one in a million didn't seem like a risk worth taking.

People in the 21st century are not technically illiterate. Children under the age of 10 all over the world own cell phones, iPods, laptop computers and other forms of technology – and they know how to use them. So when it comes to communicating the environmental risks of industrial operations, people of all ages, incomes and education levels have come to expect truth, candour, honesty and, at the same time, clarity. Communicating risk is itself a risky business. So understanding the proper way to explain those risks to those most affected is essential in maintaining constructive relationships and partnerships built on trust, respect and shared interests.

Planning... and being prepared

It's the oldest piece of advice in business: if you fail to plan you're planning to fail. You would think that more business leaders would have got the message by now.

Being in an industry where an environmental crisis is even a remote possibility requires that you plan for such a contingency. It's not altruistic or a luxury; it's simply a responsible business practice. And if you're in an industry where such a crisis is not so remote a possibility, such as electric power, chemical manufacturing or processing, pulp and paper, or other types of heavy manufacturing, failure to develop and maintain a crisis communication plan is tantamount to corporate negligence, just as an airline would be negligent if it failed to have a crisis plan for the possibility of an air disaster.

However, it's not enough to simply develop such a crisis plan. A plan needs regular testing, training, maintenance and revision. It requires a thorough analysis of all the various crisis scenarios that could occur, not just those that seem most probable. And it requires the active participation of the crisis response team and management personnel who will inevitably be charged with managing the crisis.

A key distinction should be made between crisis management and crisis communication. They are separate, but interrelated functions. Crisis managers are responsible for stabilizing an unpredictable situation. It's a lot to also ask them to assume the full burden of communication while they're immersed in the operational management of the crisis. But failure to effectively communicate during times of an environmental crisis can compound an already complex and dangerous situation. Hence the need for a separate, but interrelated crisis communications function.

When a crisis hits

Not surprisingly, most managers and executives dread crisis situations, and for good reason. A crisis is, by definition, any event or situation that, if left unmanaged, has a high probability of damaging the reputation or welfare of the organization.

But there is a rare breed of executives who take a different view. They see a crisis as an extraordinary opportunity. They believe that every problem is an opportunity to demonstrate just what kind of people and what kind of organization they really are. It's true that crises bring out the character in people and they have a habit of enabling great leaders to reveal themselves to the rest of us. Moreover, society judges the character and integrity of an organization by the way it rises to a challenge. In that respect, a crisis can be a make-or-break proposition.

Proper planning and preparation for a crisis enable an organization to seize control of media coverage and better manage the impact on its brand or reputation. Additionally, planning and skill at managing the crisis help to manage the financial impact on the organization. However, the ability to manage a crisis and bring it to a conclusion in a way that results in a positive impact on the organization's reputation hinges on its ability to communicate well. Put another way, it's seldom enough to simply manage the crisis. To truly succeed, you have to manage and communicate equally well. And the lessons from environmental crises over the past few decades have produced a roadmap from which to develop effective communication strategies.

Take control immediately

The nature of a crisis is such that by the time you first learn about it, you're already behind and in a reactive position. It's critical to respond immediately and gain control as quickly as possible in the earliest hours of the crisis. And that certainly includes communication.

The days are long gone when a next-day response in the midst of a crisis would suffice. We live in an age of instant and constant media. News breaks within seconds of an incident and is global within a matter of minutes. Within a couple of hours, wire services will have filed multiple stories, local media will have picked up the wire service feeds, filed stories on their websites and local television will be cutting into regular programming to report breaking news. With that kind of speed, it's imperative to be able to begin communicating early so that you are an integral part of the story and the best source of news and information for the media, emergency responders, local government, neighbours and the community, employees and others. The last thing you want is for all these primary target audiences to be getting their information from other sources. The only way to control rumour, fear, panic or the spread of inaccurate or misleading information is for you to be the declarative source of news and to firmly establish yourself in that role as soon as possible.

Once you are in a position to begin public communication, don't hesitate or delay. Begin the flow of accurate and timely information. Make sure that you are part of the solution to the crisis and that your communication reflects that commitment.

A very human tendency is to engage in denial. A crisis is often something that we're not prepared for and, when it strikes, it can be too overwhelming to accept. Hence, we engage in denial or disbelief. Accept only the facts as you know them, for what they are, and present them in a business-like and professional manner.

At the same time, however, it's important to put a human face and human emotion into public communication. A corporation is an impersonal thing and people are, by nature, mistrustful of the motives and priorities of businesses, particularly when an environmental crisis is involved. Regrettably, businesses today are still paying a heavy price for the legacy left them by the environmental crises of the 1970s and 1980s in terms of the level of distrust and scepticism in the media and society. Those affected want to be reassured that there are people on the front lines of the crisis who care about them, who understand their fears and concerns, and who will safeguard their interests with great care.

Apologies and the role of senior leadership

The human response should sometimes include an apology – which is where the tension with attorneys usually begins. Legal counsel will often argue, and rightly so, that public pronouncements during a crisis are subject to discovery in litigation and could be very damaging evidence before a jury. Specifically, the concern is that an apology from an executive could be interpreted as an admission of guilt or responsibility. But this isn't necessarily so.

A reasonable person could conclude that when the *Exxon Valdez* ran aground in Alaska's Prince William Sound, some kind of apology would have been appropriate. After all, here was a 1,000-foot supertanker with the Exxon corporate logo emblazoned on its hull sitting in the midst of 10 million gallons of spilled crude oil. At a minimum, some public measure of remorse for the fishermen whose livelihoods were most definitely going to be affected would have been viewed as a common courtesy. Yet there was no public response from Exxon for nearly a week after the incident.

Ashland Oil Company

In contrast to the *Exxon Valdez*, an Ashland Oil Company storage tank on the banks of the Monongahela River near Pittsburgh suddenly and without warning failed on a January night in 1988. Immediate speculation centred on the structural integrity of substandard welds and rivets that might have given way and caused the accident, sending 4 million gallons of oil flowing towards Pittsburgh. One effect of this spill was that the public water supply for the city was cut off for nearly a week.

Ashland chief executive officer John Hall flew to Pittsburgh, ignored the advice of his legal team who warned against accepting any liability for what might prove to be a subcontractor's faulty work, marched up to a group of reporters gathered at the airport and apologized to the people of Pittsburgh for the environmental impact this accident was going to have on their lives in the days ahead. The net result was nominal legal claims and fines levied against the company. But equally important is the fact that to this day, John Hall is revered as a hero in Pittsburgh for his leadership and courage in facing the community, accepting responsibility for his company's operations, and demonstrating his commitment to 'do the right thing'.

It's perfectly reasonable to be mindful of the legal concern that an apology could be interpreted as an admission of liability. But corporations that depend on the reputation of their brand for survival must be concerned not only with a court of law, but the court of public opinion. Legal liability certainly does matter, but so does the company's image, the perceptions of its customers and shareholders, the opinion of regulators and elected officials, the value of the company's brand, and its reputation as a responsible steward of the environment. For these reasons, senior management must play an active role in decision making in an environmental crisis, because it's senior management who will have to deal with the residual consequences of a failed crisis response.

There is no culpability in apologizing for the inconvenience, the disruption to daily life, the perceived threat to the environment, or other similar aspects of a crisis in cases like this. We'd expect nothing less from our neighbour if his or her tree fell on our property. An apology doesn't excuse legal or moral responsibility, but it demonstrates a human quality and a commitment to 'do the right thing' that will help preserve the value of the brand long after the crisis has passed.

There is evidence that demonstrating concern from the highest levels of the organization isn't just the right thing to do, it's also good business. On average, public companies with a reputation for being 'ethical' or that are known for their corporate social responsibility outperform the Dow Jones Industrial Average five to one over a 30-year period. The business case doesn't get much more compelling than that.

Set communication priorities

As important as it is to disseminate information to the news media, there are other target audiences whose need to know should prevail and take higher priority. In an environmental crisis, those people directly affected or impacted have the greatest need to receive information first. These are often victims whose health, safety, personal property or livelihoods are potentially at risk. They are most often the people who live closest to the facility, employees, or those who have close contact with your operations. Along with them are local emergency responders and other public authorities who are responsible for public safety and who rely on you for information.

A second tier of priority audiences are those indirectly affected by the crisis. These include other members of the community or neighbourhood, employees who might not have been onsite, customers, regulators, elected officials and local government departments.

Within this hierarchy, the news media is last. The public's need to know takes a back seat to public safety in this regard and while swift and timely communication to the news media is certainly critical, it is subordinate to those who you will depend on for help in times of crisis.

Managing a crisis and communicating within this framework of priorities illustrates once again the essential need for planning, preparation and training well in advance of a crisis.

Adopt an open, responsible public position

There's an old saying among real estate professionals that the three most important considerations in buying or selling a home are 'location, location and location'. The same idea applies to environmental crisis communications, but here the three most important considerations are 'concern, concern and concern'. Communicating your organization's genuine concern for public safety, environmental quality and the needs of those impacted by a crisis is essential to being viewed as a legitimate part of the solution, a true community partner, and an organization with real value associated with its brand.

Cooperate fully with local emergency responders, law enforcement and environmental regulators. Provide full round-the-clock assistance and support whenever and wherever it is needed. Update the news media on a regular basis. In fact, it's often helpful if you establish a regular interval for media briefings. Then stick to that schedule so that the media can easily predict when to expect new information from you.

Disclose new information promptly as it becomes available – but a cardinal rule is to only disclose the facts, without interpretation or speculation. Facts have a way of revealing themselves in bits and pieces, and what may look like the possible cause of an environmental accident on the basis of one set of facts may easily prove false hours later with the disclosure of additional facts. Meanwhile, you will have lost at least some of your credibility as a source of reliable information for the media.

If there's bad news, make sure it comes from you

Although there are exceptions to this, the experience in most environmental crises has been that if there's bad news to tell, it's most often better for that news to come from your organization rather than from another source, or worse, to withhold such information in the hope that it won't ever be disclosed.

You will always have greater control over the public disclosure of bad news if it comes from you. To be placed in a reactive position with bad news undermines your credibility and shifts the benefit of the doubt away from you because it will appear that you are attempting to conceal negative information. As recent examples, such as the Merck/Vioxx case in 2004 illustrate, the ethical and responsible course of action is to reveal to the public that which the public should know, even if nobody asks and even if you're not legally obliged.

Little things can kill you

Environmental crises are breeding grounds for communication problems and even the smallest and most trivial misstep can result in an unwanted turning point in the management of news coverage of the crisis. As in almost any crisis, it's important to keep the number of spokespeople to a minimum. Having too many voices speaking on behalf of the organization inevitably results in errors or omissions of fact, differences in judgement or understanding, or communication styles.

Confusion within the organization, usually caused by a breakdown or disruption in internal communication or lack of a clearly-defined chain of command, wreaks havoc with the efficient flow of accurate information through the organization and out to those who need to know. This can include the power struggle between communicators and legal counsel over what information can or should be disclosed, illustrating once again the need for effective planning and preparation well in advance.

Never, under any circumstance, accept rumoured or unconfirmed information as a premise of fact. As the old adage goes, 'garbage in, garbage out', and responding to a reporter's question based on rumour or a misleading premise is sure to contribute to the level of confusion or proliferation of inaccurate information.

Conclusion

Industry has made great strides in voluntarily adopting environmental stewardship as a way of doing business, and experience has shown that this new era of stewardship has been good for business and for the environment. The challenge going forward is to encourage all businesses – including those that are small, privately-held or are family businesses, or which don't have significant brand value, and even those which are not historically considered vulnerable to environmental crises – to follow a similar management model. The economics of compliance and the impact on corporate reputation can often be a very different equation in such cases, but the impact of an environmental crisis involving such companies looms just as large.

It's up to a new generation of managers, executives and owners to embrace environmental stewardship and crisis management in every corner of the business world. In that same way, it's up to communication professionals to help these organizations adapt to the way people in a 21st century society receive and interpret information about their local environment.

14 Crisis communication and the net

Is it just about responding faster... or do we need to learn a new game?

Roger Bridgeman (United States)

Introduction

The internet is accelerating the pace and scope of crises faster than ever before. A story, a rumour, a piece of information posted by a disgruntled employee becomes a 'fact' as fast as someone hits the 'send' button.

Yet, more than just a faster channel for information, the internet is a different kind of medium that is realigning the role and influence of the media, institutions and corporations, while empowering new activists and even the average citizen sitting in front of their personal computer. Today's Web 2.0 is connecting people and ideas in new ways. It's shutting down printing presses and making anyone with a Blackberry or video cell phone a new citizen journalist. It empowers even the smallest interest group to take on a global corporation.

The pace and reach of the media have always set the scope and severity of the crises that face organizations and corporations. Companies used to have a day, sometimes even a week, to respond to what the public were reading in their morning papers. Even then, the story might be restricted to the paper's circulation. Television accelerated that pace, bringing news and events into millions of homes with stark and often emotion-laden images.

So today, with the pervasiveness of the internet, with people accessing information 24/7, and with the web as a global source of news and information, is crisis communication facing a new set of challenges? Or are these just the same crisis management issues we've always faced, just moving faster?

Well, certainly the internet accelerates the pace and scope of crises faster than ever before. Yet, the internet is more than just a faster channel for information. It's a different kind of medium that is realigning the role and influence of the media, institutions and corporations, while empowering the average citizen with a computer. The internet is the first medium that promotes a new kind of interactive communication, sharing and collaboration. While the web of 15 years ago was all about sending and accessing vast amounts of information, today's Web 2.0 is about collaboration. It's about connecting people and ideas in new ways. While experienced crisis communication professionals can still apply their well-learnt principles of quick response and corporate transparency, the internet is changing the game. It's creating risk, challenges and opportunities for the public relations counsellor.

The nature of the net... fast, expansive, inclusive and a great leveller

There are certainly aspects of the web that challenge traditional crisis communication models for the public relations professional. The internet is an instant information medium that cuts both ways. A rumour, news story, changing stock price or new research all hit the web instantly, fuelling an immediate crisis with little time to respond. Or the net can be a real-time conduit for a corporate response.

The net is also a content- and media-rich channel. We get information from pictures, YouTube-posted videos, satellite images of our homes and friends' postings on MySpace. These new media have the power to convey stories in more engaging ways than printed pages. Public relations professionals are learning that responding on the web with just a press release and fact sheet doesn't work anymore. Savvy companies are responding with web-rich content such as blogs, podcasts, RSS feeds, video and links to meaningful resources.

The internet also connects people and ideas in new ways. It creates relationships and interdependencies between people and organizations that didn't exist before. Perhaps most important, the internet empowers and enlarges a company's stakeholder base, including interest and activist groups.

The internet is also a great 'information and authority leveller'. On the net everyone is an expert, their credibility isn't scrutinized and their resources are 'virtually' unlimited. While this may empower a host of new 'authorities', it creates a challenge for PR people as the sources of facts or rumours are anonymous and people's identities are easily cloaked. There's a caption to a *New Yorker Magazine* cartoon showing a dog sitting in front of a computer: 'On the internet, no one knows you're a dog.'

New medium, new risks

Our networked society, where our personal lives and business enterprises depend on being 'connected', is creating a new generation of risks that public affairs people couldn't imagine until very recently. Terms like 'hacking' and 'denial of service attacks' didn't exist a decade ago. Yet hackers who can shut down not just a website but a company's entire business enterprise represent a major new risk for today's corporation. Ask consumers what their major fear or concern about technology and big business is, and chances are they'll answer 'privacy' or 'identity theft'.

Internal e-mail and company data, usually innocuous, create new challenges. The old adage that 'anything on paper is public information' is amplified when employees are connected on the web eight hours a day. What we assumed was 'company-only' is now fodder for public debate. Even the company Christmas party innocently posted on YouTube might raise the ire of stakeholders vital to a company's business interest.

Companies are also vulnerable to copycat sites that mimic customer-facing corporate websites, posted by hackers or rouge stakeholder groups who use this technique to discredit corporations or disrupt their business. The ease with which outside groups can post and promote disinformation, and the inability of companies to locate and repudiate that information, create new challenges for PR managers in the new web-enabled society.

Today bloggers are the new investigative reporters. Companies don't fear the camera crew at the front gate as much as a blogger posting insider information, a whistle-blower's allegations, non-attributed accusations, or the unleashing of unsubstantiated rumours. Bloggers don't operate under the same standards as print journalists (they claim the information moves too fast), yet their reach and credibility grow with every hit they get and every comment they post.

Krytonite

When posts on the internet first reported that the market-leading bike lock, Krytonite, could be readily opened by inserting the plastic barrel of a ball point pen into the lock cylinder, more than 1.8 million blogs posted the news within a week. Video 'tutorials' on how to beat the lock soon went up on YouTube and other social media sites. Unprepared for the viral spread of the news, it took the company three days before it posted its first response to the web, while in the meantime trying to field hundreds of media calls.

The power to empower a crisis

The internet – the medium, the information, the power to collaborate and to share real-time information globally – is the perfect platform for creating, feeding and sustaining a crisis. Interest groups, stakeholders, disgruntled employees and labour, even competitors, can all use the medium to advance ideas and present information.

The days when social movements relied on publishing position papers, presenting at conferences or organizing demonstrations to advance their views are over. One public demonstration webcast globally, a virtual conference, or a blog touching thousands of stakeholders advances a cause faster than any other medium. These new online virtual coalitions can enlist support, raise money and demonstrate to policy players the clout of an untapped constituency. Look at how politicians have moved their campaigns and fundraising onto the web for grassroots support.

The internet puts an issue or crisis at the forefront of the public's view and policy makers' agendas. It's hard to ignore, and doesn't fade away as fast as news placed in traditional media. The net also creates virtual constituencies that can be leveraged for local grass roots initiatives or to get the attention of national policy makers. The days of the petition drive are over.

As discussed earlier, the internet is a social medium where any person or any group can convey powerful images and ideas that become impossible to trump with a simple corporate backgrounder.

News and issues, born by crisis or generated by activists, are easily networked across the internet. Traditional news expands in a linear manner (news to consumer to another consumer). The internet networks and expands information, sending news in multiple, random directions (spreading in all directions to multiple channels). The rise of citizen journalism also gives a voice to any person or organization that can post a video or 'publish' a blog. 'Mainstream' media are drawing their leads from bloggers and these citizen journalists have a reputation for being on the early edge of breaking issues and pending crises.

New tools, new opportunities

The internet offers a host of challenges, channels and opportunities for companies facing a crisis or public affairs issue. In a highly interactive and participatory medium like the web, all parties have access to new tools that create links and build communication channels that bypass traditional media, with their authority, checks and balances.

The many research and monitoring tools that we traditionally associate with the web are at the foundation of this. Certainly we have access to a host of data (almost too much) to gain an informed view on the issues impacting our companies and markets.

Mainstream search engines such as Google and Yahoo give us instant access to research, market data and, maybe, trends and issues. Yet, in the early stages of any issue or crisis, discussions and commentary will be found in the blogosphere. The next issue or crisis won't come from an editor's call, but rather from some obscure posting on a blog that ignites stakeholder passion, indignation or a call to action. Blog monitoring tools such as Google Alerts or Technorati take us from monitoring 'broadcast' media to evaluating early-warning narrow social media channels such as My Space, where issues are born and crises are fuelled.

These citizen or social media channels offer a challenge for communication professionals, especially in the midst of a crisis. There's so much chatter from an array of sources: how do you monitor, sort and assess who the opinion leaders are, and the impact they're having? Certainly the traffic and commentary on their sites is one indicator. Also, are these bloggers feeding the mainstream media and being cited as authorities by policy brokers? If they are, then PR executives, and their management, need to view these new media players as contacts in the same category as the *Wall Street Journal* and *Business Week*. In short, these blogs can act in the same way as any mainstream medium that is influencing business, government and consumer stakeholders.

Engaging the blogger community is not the typical one-way press release style of public relations. You don't 'pitch' a blogger. Effective communication is about establishing a collegial relationship where PR people can start a conversation, engage in a dialogue, or pose a question about a trend or issue. If you have a topic or idea to discuss, bring it to a blogger. If you want to promote a product, take out an ad.

The internet also fundamentally changes how people find their information. It's less about reading and sorting, and more about people requesting and filtering their information. The advent of RSS (Real Simple Syndication) feeds, now standard on many corporate sites, allows the media, stakeholders and consumers to 'request' the information they need from corporations. An RSS feed lets site visitors alert an organization that they want to receive information on a particular topic or issue. When a company issues a news release or posts a white paper or speech, that information is automatically sent to interested stakeholders. The internet provides this opportunity and savvy companies know how to feed this channel.

Communicating during a crisis in the internet age also means not just presenting facts, but helping stakeholders acquire, understand and evaluate ideas and information. A crisis website, company webinar or podcast has to present information in such a way that it helps stakeholders engage and evaluate difficult issues, not just receive the company's view. That's a challenge for PR professionals who are usually charged with 'putting out information' rather than listening, distilling and responding to stakeholder concerns. Yet that's the challenge that sets the corporate counsellor apart from just the PR practitioner.

The new ground rules

So we know during a crisis that the web requires better monitoring, a faster response and broader understanding of new media, but is that so different from traditional crisis management? Well, in a Web 2.0 world the stakeholders are now the media and they control the message and agenda. So yes, it's different.

To begin with, people's interaction with, and expectation of, the web is that information must be open, available and instant. This puts huge demands on corporations – especially during a crisis – to be responsive, open and transparent with their stakeholders. Stakeholders coming to your website, IMing executives, or responding to corporate blogs, expect immediate and candid responses to tough questions. There's no time in a crisis for a 'wait and see' strategy in the 'we expect answers now' web environment.

Additionally, a company's response during a crisis has to be more than just making sure the corporate Q&A on the website is up to date. A corporate crisis in the internet age requires a commitment and an attitude shift from a management that needs to be ready to devote their time and corporate resources to responding to stakeholders in new and immediate ways. Are they ready to blog, are senior managers prepared to cut through approval channels to get information 'up and out' quickly, and are management ready to have an online dialogue instead of posting some statement? This kind of response requires a major shift in management attitudes and processes.

One more note on transparency. The internet is unforgiving of companies that try to hide behind industry-sponsored front organizations or that have their communication people write their 'personal' blogs. When you're in an online discussion group or responding to a blog, make sure you identify yourself and stay away from defensive or corporate responses. Communicating on the net is about having a conversation, not a debate. Keep it open and honest, and web-savvy stakeholders will reward you as a trusted colleague and thought leader. Trick them just once and watch a small issue escalate into a crisis.

A standard tenet of any good crisis communication programme is anticipating and planning for a range of issues and potential crises. Working in the internet age doesn't change that principle, but the pace, scope and impact of potential crises does mean that planning is more dynamic, as is the need for a faster response. What is different is that the standard crisis plan that used to get written and then put on the shelf just doesn't work any more. The quarterly update of crisis scenarios (if that's done at all) is a model that doesn't work in the age of the internet. Monitoring the market, evaluating threats and creating worst-case scenarios become a critical and ongoing PR function, not a quarterly assignment.

Part of that process is the kind of deep monitoring that the web allows and demands. It also means breaking down corporate silos so that reports from the field about trends, customer comments, competitive information, what's being 'heard on the street', etc, become integrated into the corporate management function. Responding to a crisis on the internet may require breaking down traditional chain-of-command corporate hierarchies in order to collect insightful stakeholder-level information. In-depth monitoring has to be more than just the PR intern scanning the web for clips and blog postings.

The speed of the internet, and its content-rich channels, means that corporations need to be ready to provide more and more information, in multiple media and formats. A decade ago savvy companies were creating 'in-the-ready' web pages, or 'dark pages', to post during emergencies. Today, that content has to include podcasts from executives, video clips and animated graphics explaining complex technologies. A crisis response site needs dynamic resource links and click-to-phone links to the senior communication professional. Yet today, most websites don't even list a phone number for their PR contact, just an arm's length 'PRContact@companyABC' e-mail link. In the internet age, that's the same as providing a 'No comment'.

Crisis communication – engagement versus pronouncements

Managing a crisis in an internet-empowered environment demands that we think and act differently than the crisis communication models of just a decade ago. While communication, by its nature, is always two-way, the internet requires that our communication and response during a crisis are more of a conversation than a statement. It's more of an engagement than a pronouncement. Traditional crisis communication models talk about 'getting out our story', and marshalling our spokespeople and third-party experts to project our point of view. On the internet, it's all about engaging with our stakeholders, the new lords of social media.

So, in the middle of a crisis, how do we engage with our supporters and detractors alike? Let's take a lesson from the interest groups and advocacy stakeholders who do such a good job in engaging their communities. To begin with, make it personal. Get rid of the corporate speak and (dare I say) PR-polished prose. Get your senior executives out in front, have them open their blogs, engage in in-person and online town meetings, and craft their messages that say, 'We understand, here's what we're doing' and maybe more important, 'Here is how you can help.'

There's certainly a risk here. All communication on the net involves risk. We invite people to respond to our blogs, but what might they say? Can we control the message? Will whatever we say, with the best intentions, get twisted and manipulated by the opposition? Probably. Yet the internet, for all its liabilities, offers a new venue for presenting an open and honest response and, regardless of a company's position, its innocence or culpability in a crisis, the public will respond to a direct and open dialogue with a company. The internet offers both tools and opportunities for this new dialogue.

Conclusion

So, if we look at traditional, pre-internet models of communication, especially during a corporate crisis, we see classic 'unidirectional' models of communication. We send, people receive, we listen, we evaluate, and re-send ... pretty linear. Working a crisis in Web 2.0 is more like trying to connect an array of dots.

This new dynamic requires corporations to find, engage with, and share ideas with total strangers. Some are friends, some foes, but most are stakeholders just trying to figure out which side of the road to travel. Corporate communication professionals have a unique opportunity to chart a new course, reaching out to and 'asking for directions' from a community of stakeholders who, in the midst of a crisis, are empowered by the web to help a company get back on track.

In traditional crisis communication, corporations react and present information. On the internet, stakeholders look for information, ideas and a meaningful exchange. Corporations need to meet that challenge by responding and engaging in new ways. It's what communication is supposed to be: listening and sharing, not just talking.

15 Organizational barriers to crisis and public affairs management

If we know what to do, why do we keep getting it wrong?

Roger Bridgeman (United States)

Introduction

Public relations can harness a set of core communication tenets that can guide companies through crises and public affairs challenges. Quick response, open disclosure, listening to stakeholders and responding to our communities are all guideposts for good corporate communication.

So, if companies know what they're supposed to do, why do so many organizations still stumble when faced with a crisis? The answer may lie in common management attitudes that still prevail in many organizations. Problems vary from responding too late, through underestimating the scope of the issue, to a misguided self-confidence that corporate resources and facts can overwrite public perception and passion. There is the senior executive who holds back the truth, tarnishing the reputation of his or her company; the company whose slow response creates public panic and pain; a product recall that's delayed; questionable financial dealings and 'opaque transparency'.

Crisis communication is one of the most studied and analysed corporate disciplines chronicled in a business manager's textbook. We study the Tylenol crisis, read how to deal with natural disasters, watch the ethical mistakes of corporate executives, and review the checklists for good corporate social responsibility. The public relations profession has a core set of communication guidelines that tell practitioners how to counsel their companies and clients during crises and public affairs challenges. This chapter examines some of the common organizational pitfalls that public relations professionals can watch out for, to help their companies manage when faced with the next crisis or public affairs stumble.

Dismissing the issue, marginalizing the opposition

'Who are those "nuts" at the door?'

A major accident at a plant, a storm that wreaks havoc, product-related injuries or a recall. These are all crises that can't be ignored and management understands the need to marshal resources and move quickly and decisively.

But what about those crises that are just starting to percolate? Not a full-blown crisis; just an issue that seems confined to a particular area or stakeholder group. Even when these issues explode on to the national or international scene, it's sometimes too easy for management to dismiss either the issue or the group. You've heard it: 'These people just have an agenda, ignore them and their issue goes away. Respond and we just feed the fire.'

A common challenge that PR professionals often face is management's all-too-eager desire to dismiss the crisis or issue as short-term and inconsequential or to underestimate the stakeholders behind the issue and dismiss their agenda. Sometimes it's easy to understand why. Perhaps the issue seems small, insignificant, or maybe even 'silly'.

There's a new movement in Europe that is taking a stand against 'eating fast'. If you're a multi-billion dollar fast food chain, this may look like a bunch of folks on the fringe who hate eating greasy fast food. Or maybe this movement is really a response against the US notion of 'fast' everything. An astute PR person may see in this the underpinnings of an anti-US movement rebelling against our cultural influence on Europe. (Who can blame them? Just look at the TV programming we blast overseas.)

What's the impact of 'slow eating'? Well it's tough for fast food chains to break into new markets, and it changes their entire economic model when they have fewer customer 'turns' and have to build larger facilities to accommodate more people. Yet, it's easy to imagine how the fast food industry at first readily dismissed this brewing crisis as just something on the fringe.

The job of the public relations professional is to keep an eye on these issues, big and small, and help management understand and assess the business risks and opportunities. Which ones do we watch? When do we respond? How do we react in the best interest of our companies and our stakeholders?

Another common pitfall occurs when management tries to underestimate or devalue the issue or group by 'name calling' and stereotyping them. Even my use of the term 'fringe' implies that a problem doesn't merit serious attention. Who needs to pay attention to anything labelled as 'fringe'? It's the same thing when we label those 'tree-hugging environmentalists'. Yet, the Sierra Club is one of the largest private organizations in the United States. Our friends and neighbours are members. Can we readily dismiss them?

So in the midst of a crisis or brewing issue, management want to dismiss the groups with labels such as 'fringe', 'non-mainstream' or even 'the left' or 'the right', as if we can somehow marginalize these groups with a label. In fact, interest groups often represent the mainstream, and are well organized, focused and able to deliver their clout and constituencies to fuel a crisis or respond to an issue.

Management often underestimate the influence and impact of these groups, but they know how to use new media and citizen journalism, while corporations are just trying to figure out how to post a once-a-month blog for the CEO. Their media and legislative contacts help them make plenty of noise. Sure, maybe this issue may fade, but these groups know how to make their case to the public in a way that has long-term ramifications.

Averting a crisis by early action

'I'm sorry, I wasn't listening. What did you say?'

A crisis sometimes literally explodes on to the scene. Yet in most cases there are usually early warning signs, small embers of concerns that are fanned into a flame.

A major and vexing problem for corporate management is trying to listen, or 'pay attention' at the early stages of these issues before they become a crisis. These potential early stage warnings are, in fact, exactly the time when change and action can mitigate a crisis.

Often, responding to the concern early on can avert a crisis. If a consumer privacy group is targeting financial services companies for their handling of consumer data, then taking early action by creating a consumer Bill of Rights, or deploying advanced security technology, might stem the impact of this issue. This kind of response requires valuable corporate resources and capital, yet it's a minor investment compared with having to respond to government regulatory intervention or a consumer boycott and the impact on a company's stock price.

Early monitoring and response to a potential crisis can also give an organization enough time to calculate, respond and maybe even co-opt an issue before it turns into a crisis. If a healthcare provider is seeing the winds of change regarding, say, access to hospital care statistics, it might decide to 'own' the issue, putting in place policies and public access systems that get it ahead of the curve. This kind of forward thinking can give the healthcare provider a competitive position in its market.

The days of annual corporate responsibility reviews or issues mapping, monthly legislative monitoring and weekly clips reports are over. Today's public relations people need to monitor, in real-time, the new channels of their stakeholders from blogs and 24/7 international news, new media and citizen journalism.

The irony of early monitoring is that in collecting so much information it may be difficult to identify these early, pre-crisis issues. Most large companies face hundreds of these issues – from public advocacy, through legislative affairs, to workplace rights. Which one should the PR professional focus on? How do you track all these changes going on among your stakeholders? How can you alert management to these potential concerns? The challenge is setting up a process to identify, review and re-evaluate these issues and to constantly keep management aware of the business and policy implications of these potential threats (or opportunities).

Corporate resources can't trump a crisis

'Put the lawyers and PR guys on this.'

Business people are action-oriented. They see a challenge, set a strategy, assign resources to a problem, and look for 'checklist' efficiency in executing the tactics. Once an action or campaign is set in motion, they move on to the next challenge, assuming this week's problem is being managed.

But a crisis never works that way. Crises evolve, their agendas change and expand, and the stakeholders involved are constantly reshaping the game and recalculating their moves. It's not unlike how companies are constantly responding to a competitive situation where every corporate action is met with a counter-response by other market players.

A crisis should be no different. Yet many senior executives, by assigning their legal and public affairs team to a problem, compartmentalize the issue. This creates a potentially dangerous, high-liability problem: the misconception that marshalling corporate resources can solve public perception problems.

It's a common attitude that corporate resources – people, time, expertise, money, resources – can trump an issue or gloss over a potential crisis. We want to influence some legislation and start a lobbying campaign. A corporate financial crisis is revealed, and we head to the court and issue a press release. We think that lawyers and PR people can fix these issues, and once we initiate a legal response, or have the PR people run articles and place paid advocacy ads, that we've got this situation fixed. In fact, what is needed during a crisis is meaningful response and a committed management team looking not just at the immediate crisis or issue, but taking a hard look at their internal corporate governance and business processes.

Responding to a crisis with real process change

'It's about a fix, not a change.'

Many companies facing real business challenges, issues such as consumer boycotts or regulatory intervention, often find out the hard way that the real solution to an issue needs to be driven at a senior management level. Solutions may even involve changes in fundamental management attitudes and internal business processes.

Nike

Nike found this out a decade ago when it faced charges of worker abuse at its subcontractor facilities in Asia. It received bad press, lots of consumer threats, and was faced with possible legal and regulatory actions. Its well-intentioned response was to put into place, and publicize, a new set of corporate workplace standards. The problem was that this response existed mostly on paper, with very little inspection of its vendor sites, and no real repercussions for its manufacturing partners who failed to comply.

The company did try to fix the problem, but eventually it had to go all the way into its procurement processes to make changes. It stopped the practice of short-term, six-month contracts with suppliers, which was creating a negative incentive for its partners to push their workers to meet higher and higher productivity demands. Nike changed its procurement processes to build long-term relationships with its suppliers that offered incentives for them to make, and afford, long-term improvements in worker conditions.

Once faced with this issue, Nike had to make fundamental business process and management changes, not just institute some PR policy. What was the cost in terms of implementation and lost business opportunity, not to mention their stock price, while it worked through these fundamental business issues?

Assuming a quick fix will make the problem go away

'When it looks like it's over, it's just begun.'

The Nike example illustrates that there are no quick fixes during a crisis or issues-management situation and that the problem rarely completely resolves itself.

Many companies have a false sense of resolution. They think that by responding with some PR programme, such as posting information on the web, hosting an informational webinar, taking out an ad, or maybe patching up community relations with a charitable donation, will somehow fix the problem. They're ready to move on to the next challenge, without really understanding the root of the problem, the public perception liability they've created or the long-term opportunity this offers for interest in advocacy groups.

Companies may try to recover from a crisis by setting up an education programme, or posting educational information on their site. Yet the issue will remain in the public view, and will likely morph and expand because that's how interest groups keep the issue and their agenda current.

These interest groups are just doing in their own communication and advocacy what corporations often do in their own marketing – reinventing themselves. Companies revise their product or service, they modify and re-launch their product to meet changing market conditions, all in an attempt to keep their product relevant and interesting to customers. Interest groups do the same thing by charting social and policy changes, responding with a new issue and agenda and reinvigorating their outreach communication to keep the crisis and issue in front of the public and policy makers.

Public relations practitioners face the unpopular task of reminding their management that crises linger and change. Monitoring and constantly reassessing these issues, and assigning valuable corporate resources to the problem, is the cost of remaining vigilant.

Confusing facts with perception

'If they could just understand the facts.'

How often do we hear, 'If we could just make these people understand they'd see how wrong they are'? In the business world we work with facts, but in the sphere of public affairs we deal with perceptions.

Business people make their living from presenting information and persuading people to their point of view. They use facts and figures, research and data, testimonials from satisfied customers, all to convince colleagues, partners and customers that their position is right. Yet when faced with crisis-laden video pictures, blogs gone wild, interest groups presenting their information (or disinformation) across new media, companies don't know how to respond. They issue releases and fact sheets while the other side is delivering sound bites and emotional videos.

Facts are important, but companies need to speak in human terms, understanding the emotion of the issues, not just the facts. Find people to tell your story, get executives out of their offices and in front of their stakeholders. Speak in terms that say, 'We understand', and help management appreciate that what people believe affects business far more than what is in a white paper or fact sheet.

Combating the corporate siege mentality

'Hey, we're the good guys – right?'

Most companies have lots of good people doing good things. They make great products, employ people, pay taxes and involve themselves with the local community. So during a crisis when someone says, 'You're wrong, you're the bad guys', a company's reaction is personal, and management either want to lash out or head to the bunker. When a crisis occurs, the public looks for answers to hard questions and for someone to blame. It's a tough and emotional time for executives. The usual response is restrained anger and an orderly retreat back into the corporate castle, or the 'war room', where companies fall into a 'them against us' siege mentality. Executives surround themselves with consultants who tell them they're right and they can beat back this crisis.

This situation usually yields that negative, 'We've got to beat them to win' attitude that generates negative action and communication. Legal action, union strikes and public battles fought in the press all create an environment that is impossible to back away from and leave residual stakeholder resentment for a company and its products.

The other challenge of a siege mentality is that it doesn't recognize alternatives or moderate views, or sometimes, even notions of compromise. A siege mentality breeds a 'win or lose' approach, not listening and accommodation. Yet during a crisis is exactly the time companies need to be listening hard, considering all options and points of view. This may be the time for some kind of compromise or rethinking of an entrenched business practice. A crisis can offer a chance to look at 'What about this?' options or, 'They might have a point of view worth considering.' It's a more creative option than retreating behind a corporate wall. Once again it's the PR professionals' sometimes unpopular task to present management with alternative points of view, to suggest new ideas, or to seek a compromise in a difficult 'win or lose' corporate environment.

Conclusion

If we look at many of these common crisis concerns, the core of the managerial issues is more of an emotional response than a strategic lapse. The role of the public relations professional, then, is to be the counsellor who spots these organizational symptoms early and presents management with a view that moves past a short-term crisis toward an understanding of the long-term interest – one that articulates both shareholder and stakeholder values and a view that balances the bottom line with open and engaging communication during and well after any crisis.

16 Risk managers

New leaders in crisis communication?

Odile Vernier (France)

Introduction

The job of risk manager is a fairly new one. It was originally focused on assessing the risks linked to a company's activity and on how to limit or eliminate those risks. But it soon became apparent that the communication aspect had to be included and coordinated with the communication manager and consulting firms that specialize in crisis communication.

While risk managers initially managed insurance-related risks, their job is becoming increasingly important in companies as they are called on to manage corporate communication as well. This is as much due to the various laws that call for more transparency (the Sarbannes–Oxley act in the United States, new requirements on corporate governance in France, etc) as it is due to the financial risks that threaten a brand and its reputation.

The risk manager's main mission is to identify and reduce the impact that a random business risk could have on a company's finances and future development. This includes hazard-related risks (accidents, theft, fires, accidental pollution, etc) and all the threats related to brand damage and its effect on the company.

The risk manager's mission, as defined by AMRAE, the French risk management association includes:

Identifying the main risks that could likely affect a company's financial position and performance; ensuring that all subsidiaries have the technical management and training necessary for reducing risks; negotiating and managing the company's financial and insurance coverage; supervising and simplifying insurance programmes when managed by the subsidiaries. Communication and risk prevention are an integral part of the duties of a risk manager, who works closely with the director of communication.

The risk manager participates in corporate communication that deals with practical issues related to managing crises like product recalls, and is increasingly involved in managing risks related to public opinion. The risk manager's role is gaining such importance that it sometimes takes over the communication department either by supervising it, or by working with its management. To understand this evolution – no, initially it was not a new profession trying to define and conquer territory within businesses – it is important to review the new emerging threats that can impinge on brands.

When brands do not measure up to public opinion

Companies today have made considerable progress in the area of communication, which is more often than not constructive and has enabled them to establish stable relations with the public around them. Motivated by what is at stake in such relations, companies strive to comply with the 'information requirements' that modern day management and the law demand. Companies open up and present themselves publicly, and information procedures have multiplied. But are they listening as well? Often companies are so busy listening to themselves that they can't really hear anything else! In the absence of publicly expressed opinions, they are oblivious to public opinion and this is where they get lost.

Versatile, forgetful, generous, quick to flare up, public opinion demands that facts be accounted for immediately, effectively and, depending on the criteria, sometimes unrealistically for a business. Companies have their rules; public opinion has its convictions. Companies claim the right to evolve freely in the legislative framework that applies to them. Public opinion claims the right to have control over and punish 'abusive' situations. One is backed up by the law, the other by morals.

Convinced of their own truth, companies do not (or only dimly) perceive the often profound changes in public opinion. Blinded by its virtuous quest, public opinion refuses to recognize the rights of companies, which are theirs by law.

'Social autism'

There have been many cases in the past where companies have had to pay dearly for discovering the power of public opinion too late. Even now, many seem afflicted by 'social autism' that cuts them off from constructive dialogue with the public. They believe what they say and do not hear what they are being told.

For instance, most of the pharmaceutical industry's communication is out of phase with public opinion. When this industry desperately tries to promote a humanistic profile dedicated to research in the interest of the public, public opinion and institutions reflect back to it a cold, dehumanized image of research and private profit. There is a total lack of understanding here, which will lead to rejection.

Similarly, the food and agriculture sector risks paying dearly for its incapacity to take seriously into account public opinion's growing indignation at escalating child obesity. By making out the consumer to be the 'guilty' party ('Our products are good but you don't use them correctly'), the industry locks itself into a logic that negates its own excesses and only 'feeds' general suspicion.

Turning public opinion into an asset

It is time companies considered managing public opinion with the same focus as other business strategies. It is not completely uncharted territory.

Large international groups have already immersed themselves in a frantic policy of dialogue with their various publics or 'stakeholders', which opens the way to managing public opinion in real-time. 'Social reports' publish ethical quotas, and moves toward sustainable development are increasing.

French businesses, with the support of professional managers of public opinion, are initiating their cultural revolution. In this respect, communication has a major role to play. It is the only way to ensure that a company's fate is not suspended during public opinion's unpredictable twists and turns.

It is imperative that companies gain awareness of this state of affairs, for contrary to generally accepted ideas, public opinion cannot be fought. Either companies adapt because they've understood how it works or they disappear. All companies know the risks. The acceleration of technological progress, rapid changes in our societies as well as the speed that information travels, all increase these risks substantially. Numerous companies know that a crisis can be very expensive and even destroy a business. The job of risk manager was created to define risks better and to arbitrate between the different investment priorities within a strategy of risk prevention.

The brand – its financial and social implications

Lately, many large single-brand groups have developed, for example Danone, Samsung, Shell and Electrolux. This gives these groups the advantage of making considerable savings when it comes to marketing and advertising, but also makes them more vulnerable to attack.

Brand value is now included on company balance sheets. For example, according to the Interbrand classification, Samsung went from a valuation of US $5.2 billion in 2000 and 43rd position, to a valuation of US $16.6 billion and 20th position. While this can be attributed to the brand's successful globalization efforts, again, it also makes it increasingly vulnerable.

Coca-Cola

For the number one brand, Coca-Cola, with a valuation of US $67 billion (2006 Interbrand classification), the slightest slip has immediate repercussions. In 1998, there was a crisis of confidence in the product in Belgium and France due to reports that drinks cans had been contaminated. Production at the Dunkirk factory was suspended as was distribution of the cans for a couple of days, which had immediate financial consequences. The loss was estimated as being US $350 million, and a sudden drop in the share price on the NYSE.

A year later, after a long investigation, the Pasteur Institute proved that the cans had not been contaminated, but the damage was done. Coca-Cola's confidence index with French consumers plummeted, as it fell from 5th position to 21st position. Brand risk led to financial risk in the strict sense of the term. This is the sort of situation that resulted in the growing importance of the risk manager's role.

Risks, risk managers and crisis communication

Image, opinion and reputation

Before assessing risks, it is imperative to be fully aware of the various parts of the company's brand image, and the factors tolerated – or not – by the publics affected by the brand, bearing in mind that brand awareness is not an exact science.

Brand image consists of diverse elements such as financial results, performance, ethics, governance, social policies, etc. None of these is stable. They can all quickly fluctuate, depending on the group (share-holders, consumers, associations, public opinion, or employees) reacting to the image, as there are many differences of perception among these groups.

Beyond assessing its image, a company also needs to become aware of its reputation, that is to say, the sum of all the different ways its image is perceived. Risks can be identified when evaluating all these elements. There are three types of risk:

1. Those directly related to the company's business: social policy, governance, the quality of products made or of services rendered, environmental policies, etc.
2. Those related to company actions that go against company core values. The pharmaceutical industry, for one, vaunts noble values that serve humanity and finds itself in the dock for abandoning activities that aren't profitable or not mentioning the side-effects of certain products.
3. Those related to company actions that go against the values of the times. Take for example, a subject that is worldwide in scope, that of obesity. The food and agriculture industry is quite vulnerable to a risk related to this issue.

It is important that a company draws up a list of vulnerability points. Those in charge of corporate communication and risk managers will need to permanently update this list. It goes without saying that the list will have to be adapted to each country where the company oper-ates, since sensitivity and values can vary significantly from one country to another.

When recently asked how to best manage a crisis, a client of Beau Fixe replied, 'You need a good communication agency and a good insurance company!' The cost of crises has skyrocketed since the 1980s, not only because they have multiplied, but also because the overall globalization of activities, markets and the media brings about a globalization of the crisis (see Figure 16.1). An incident that takes place in a small area and which, in the past, could easily have been contained (with costs limited to damages and repair) is now blown out of proportion on a worldwide scale, with commensurate costs.

Here are some cases in point. (Please note that the information given here is pertinent to France.)

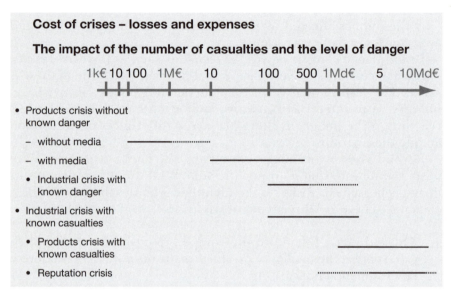

Figure 16.1 An exponential inflation in the cost of crises

Bridgestone & Firestone tyres (2000)

- Tyre blowouts (200 deaths and more than 500 hurt) – 1,400 complaints filed in 2002.
- 6.5 million tyres recalled.
- Net profits divided by 4 between 1999 and 2000.
- Share value fell by 60 per cent.

Automobile manufacturers

- Regular recalls in this industry.
- Average recall – 100,000 vehicles for an average cost of €50 million.

Camembert cheese contaminated by listeria and salmonella (March 1999)

- 25,000 products recalled (or 5,000 according to some sources).
- An immediate drop in sales of 75 per cent.
- A 14.5 per cent loss of market share – nine months later, pre-crisis sales level regained (reaching about 25 per cent of the market).

Bayer drug recall (Baycol, Staltor and Cholstat) August 2001

- Financial consequences – share price fell by 43 per cent.
- Consequences on the operating result: a 6.5 per cent decline in sales figures for the 2002 first quarter and a 46 per cent drop in operating profit.
- Legal consequences: 40,000 patients filed complaints in the United States, which led to 600 trials. In France, 400 complaints were filed at the end of 2001.

Faced with this sort of situation, the company and its risk manager must take into account the limits of its insurance coverage. In fact, today, insurance policies essentially cover four fields:

1. Product recalls.
2. Crisis management costs, that is, reimbursement of those expenses related to maintaining company market share (communication, advertising, working to get outlets to continue to distribute the product).
3. Legal liability.
4. Assets.

Some additional risks are partially covered by a few companies up to an amount that varies from €2 million to €25 million. These are loss of brand image (in France, in our experience, there is only one insurance product on the market, developed by AGF (Allianz group) and Beau Fixe); loss or decrease in sales figures; and personal liability of managers and social agents. Items not covered by such policies are:

- ongoing loss of confidence;
- loss of market share;
- loss of stock market value;
- R&D expenses necessary to recuperate the three previous items.

Of course, it is just these, the most costly risks, that are not covered by insurance companies and which could drive a company out of business. Faced with this situation and other dramatic examples in the 1990s and the early 2000s (Enron, Andersen, Parmalat, etc) risk managers of large organizations found themselves faced with the necessity of having to coordinate with company spokespeople.

The implications of recent events give renewed meaning to prevention and management of crisis communication. Where before communications departments focused solely on boosting the brand image, without necessarily taking into account the overall stakes for a company, adding risk managers to the picture will give companies a big-picture strategy.

The main advantage is to expand the company vision and make it more all-encompassing. The crisis management team is in a better position to anticipate super-crises and to take into account the destabilizing factors that crisis management itself implies.

Crises need to be handled in real-time

Because of the new forms of media like blogs, forums, e-mails and text messages that allow consumers, citizens and employees to broadcast and receive all sorts of information, crisis management can no longer completely control the situation. For Christophe Roux Dufort, Professor of Strategic Management at the Management School in Lyons, France, when a crisis occurs, the speed that information travels greatly exceeds the capacity of companies to deal with it:

> Moreover, the information gets distorted as it rapidly spreads. What is worse, the new forms of media lead their users to believe in their perfect transparency, which is an illusion, while company communication is regarded with suspicion.

In order to act quickly, it is imperative to prioritize targets and to make certain choices. It is unrealistic to think that the company can deal with all the targets at once. Moreover, it is necessary to plan upstream for the organization to have a robust IT infrastructure in place to deal with congested servers and also to mobilize the human resources necessary to answer the huge number of e-mails pouring in. As an example, when the Michelin-equipped teams refused to participate in the Formula 1 US Grand Prix in June 2005, visits to the Michelin internet site multiplied by eight. The company received 2,000 e-mails in a week, when normally it receives 1,000 per year on this subject. This suggests that companies may even want to step up their corporate communication to corporate interaction.

Company governance: a new source of crises

It is not easy to define company governance; it probably varies from one country to the next. Generally speaking, we can attempt to define it as a renewed shareholder counter-power. It is as much based on more active board roles as it is a way for shareholders to monitor companies. It is a type of management that looks after shareholder value and actively participates in meetings and possible legal proceedings as a means of taking care of shareholders' rights.

Company governance can be thought of as a balance between unconditional shareholder power and managerial excesses. Here is a quote about governance as seen by the French. A French company's management 'see it as a means of contesting through which their authority is put into question by Anglo-Saxon troublemakers, and reported by ignorant journalists and conference organizers at a loss for real ideas'.

Despite the resistance of some company leaders, company governance has become a new source of crises for which organizations and risk managers are not always prepared and often find themselves at a loss to respond. Companies as well known as Suez, Carrefour, Shell and Vinci have all recently experienced this. The following illustrates how brand risk is more and more linked to financial risk.

The US Sarbannes–Oxley financial transparency act is applicable to all US company subsidiaries throughout the world. However, applying this law, especially in Europe, is not all that easy. For example, in France it clashes with the policies of the CNIL (Commission Nationale de Informatique et des Libertés). Beau Fixe has had to intervene twice this year for subsidiaries of US groups when their factories went on strike, pitting French law against US law, calling on support from the CNIL. A solution was reached with the French authorities. Only recently, both Dupont de Nemours and McDonalds were judged in France on this subject. We are sliding toward more and more legal hearings, which is not going to simplify matters. This is just another reason why risk management skills are increasingly important for businesses today.

The risk manager, director of communication and public relations consulting agency now make up a trio that works to preserve company image and reputation. The speed with which information travels, the rising number of communication outlets, as well as the exorbitant cost of crises all make this an inescapable step for the future of numerous companies throughout the world.

Conclusion

It could have been dangerous to have sensitive matters or crisis communication handled by various risk managers, communication managers or consulting firms. Indeed, there could have been a risk in sharing responsibilities, and delays in decision making could have occurred. Nevertheless, somehow it works pretty well. There's no single model that defines each one's responsibility because patterns differ from one company to another – but they work. However, this does mean that all crises are well handled. There are good times ahead for consulting firms.

17 Crisis communication checklists

Peter Frans Anthonissen (Belgium)

Crisis-control list
1. Preparations

- What crises could confront our company?
- What public groups and stakeholders do we have to take into consideration?
- How can we communicate with them?
- What do we tell them?
- Who will be on the crisis team and the crisis communication team?
- What are our options?
- Are the members of the crisis team and our spokespeople trained sufficiently?
- Do we know how to deal with stress properly?
- What crisis manual do we use?
- Can it be used in practice?
- Do we have contact with our public groups and stakeholders?

Crisis-control list
2. Public groups and stakeholders

Below you will find an overview of the most common public groups. This list should be augmented in accordance with the needs of your company. For the public group 'relevant ministries', for example, you will have to investigate yourself which ministries are important to your company. This list is not complete, of course. Investigate who could be among your public groups.

- Media: international/national
  - print media, general and specialist;
  - TV;
  - radio;
  - news magazines;
  - internet: e-zines, websites.
- Media: local
  - general newspapers and corporate publications;
  - TV;
  - radio.
- Trade press.
- Government:
  - relevant ministries;
  - other government services;
  - members of parliament;
  - provincial administrations.
- Local government and emergency services:
  - municipal administrations;
  - police;
  - hospitals;
  - fire brigade.

Do not forget that police, fire brigades and other emergency services often have their own communication services. Such organizations also have an interest in not keeping facts secret because they could themselves be affected negatively.

- Company:
  - personnel;
  - if the company is part of a group: head office, parent company, branches;
  - employee organizations;
  - lawyers;

- insurance companies;
- shareholders;
- investment companies;
- clients;
- competitors;
- suppliers;
- employer organizations and professional associations.
- Miscellaneous:
  - family members;
  - neighbourhood residents;
  - environmental associations, pressure groups, non-governmental organizations (NGOs).

General or public opinion is also a public group and can be reached indirectly via communication with another public group such as the media, or directly via online information on your own website.

Crisis-control list
3. Crisis centre

Major international companies have their own crisis centres that are equipped with everything imaginable. For many companies, such a set up is financially unfeasible. Nevertheless, every company should take some minimum precautions. The more prepared a company is, the easier it will be to get a crisis under control. Those who are prepared will not be disturbed during the crisis with irrelevant telephone calls; people know where they need to go; and there will always be recording equipment available to record news reports.

Some items to consider:

- Crisis room and crisis-communication room: a meeting room in the company itself? A hotel in the neighbourhood? A specially equipped room?
- Alternative crisis rooms and crisis-communication rooms (for example in the event of fire, explosion, inaccessibility of the buildings, such as during sit-ins.)
- Mobile telephones and personal digital assistants.
- Guarded access.
- A suitable area and furnishings for the crisis team, crisis-communication team and others.

- Some telephones, including one telephone with a secret outside line.
- Computer with e-mail and internet access.
- Fax equipment.
- Material to view/listen to TV and radio messages (and contact with the press agency).
- An area to prepare TV or radio interviews.
- ISDN line to transmit video conferences, images and interviews.
- Writing paper, pens and pencils.
- The capability to send out mailings quickly (on paper or by e-mail).
- Log book to record all actions taken.
- Support: press and TV monitoring, text typing, dissemination, etc.
- Equipment to record telephone calls.
- Soft drinks, coffee and tea, snacks, etc (catering service that is available 24 hours a day).
- Provision to spend the night at the company site (or close by).
- A separate room to receive the media (preferably in the company and as close as possible to the entrance).

Crisis-control list
4. What's in your crisis-communication survival kit?

What should every member of the crisis-communication team always have close at hand? Think of things that are essential for someone who is away from the company site and who must speak to the media.

Here are some suggestions:

- Crisis manual and sufficient information on the background to the crisis situation.
- Essential telephone numbers.
- Media list with names and addresses of journalists.
- Mobile telephones, digital personal assistants and chargeable batteries.
- Telephone cards.
- Portable PC.
- Writing paper, pens and pencils.
- Tape recorder, Dictaphone (and tapes).
- Radio.

- Portable TV.
- Wristwatch with alarm function.
- Reserve batteries.
- Sufficient money.
- Credit cards and bank cards.

Crisis-control list
5. Background information

Every member of the crisis-communication team must be prepared for questions from the media or other groups. Ensure that every member has sufficient information about the company:

- Information on the company: size, products, sector, history, figures, number of employees, etc.
- Production processes and/or methods.
- Detailed information on the products and services.
- Chemicals and/or other materials: which ones? What are they used for? Why are they necessary?
- Safety and quality: point out the good reputation of the company. What investments have been made? What quality controls are in place?
- Location: history of the company/factory/organization.
- All other information that can be useful for the company.

Ensure that the information is available in clear language (avoid jargon and explain abbreviations) and structured in such a way that a busy journalist can understand the most important information easily and can process it properly.

Also give the journalists graphics, organizational diagrams, photographs, film and video material, PowerPoint presentations and similar material that they can use to illustrate their broadcast, article or report. That way, your own material gets published.

Crisis-control list
6. Employee training: dealing with the media

Teach your employees how they should respond in crisis situations, how they should deal with journalists, when they are not authorized to speak to journalists, etc. Regularly scheduled training is not a disposable luxury!

They should pay attention to the following things:

- Give no details – not even your name. Don't let yourself get dragged into a conversation.
- Always assure the journalist that you will pass his or her questions on immediately to a spokesperson who is aware of the situation and who will call him or her back right away.
- Ensure that you find out the following:
  - Who are you talking to? What is his or her name?
  - What is his or her position?
  - On behalf of which newspaper or broadcaster is he or she calling?
  - What is his or her telephone number?
  - What does he or she want to know?
- Give the message and all the information that you have learnt to an authorized person immediately. Check whether the spokesperson actually contacted the journalist.
- Always be polite and patient. That is the message and will remain so, even – and particularly – in difficult circumstances.

It is not enough for you to give this list to your employees. Explain things to them and schedule regular training sessions.

Crisis-control list
7. Crisis manual

Do not write this manual alone – teamwork is required. Writing it is the job of the crisis team and the crisis-communication team. Your crisis manual must be a reference work for meetings, brainstorming sessions, crisis training and simulations. Every company has different needs.

Here is a suggested list of contents for a good crisis manual:

- Introduction: short description of what is expected of the members of the crisis team and the crisis-communication team; company philosophy; how to use the manual.
- Procedures: short description of the procedure to be followed in the event of a crisis in the company.
- Crisis team and crisis-communication team: the names and positions of the members of the teams; brief description of their responsibilities; telephone numbers of the team members and external advisers such as lawyers, PR consultants, etc (office number and a mobile or private number that they can be reached on, day and night); detailed information on their back-ups in case a member of the team is ill, on vacation or simply unreachable.
- Public groups: list of the public groups, with addresses and telephone numbers of contact people; emergency numbers of government services, hospitals, emergency services, ministries, lawyers.
- Message: summary of what should/can be communicated to the outside world in the event of a crisis: who, what, where, when, why and how.
- Material: the crisis centre (location) and similar information; what material is provided, for whom is it intended and where it can be found; user instructions available.
- Media: checklist with media-relations principles, how to prepare for interviews and give interviews successfully.
- Background information: brochures on the company, products, procedures, etc. Technical information can sometimes be useful, too.
- Useful addresses and telephone numbers: press-monitoring services, caterers, etc.

Crisis-control list
8. How to handle a crisis

Some general principles:

- Don't stand by idly waiting... do something... take action.
- Always repeat the same message.
- Call the crisis team and the crisis-communication team together immediately and sequester them.
- Evaluate the situation (see control list 9).

- Decide which strategy should be followed.
- Identify the public groups and stakeholders affected.
- Determine what you want to communicate to the outside world; if possible, determine who the opinion leaders are.
- Prepare a plan and carry it out.
- Inform those who should be informed.
- Centralize all incoming and outgoing information.
- Understand your public groups and speak their language.
- Give information quickly and clearly.
- Calm everyone down.
- Respond to negative reporting.
- Be flexible and creative.
- Think long term and keep the reputation of your company and organization always at the forefront of your thoughts.

Crisis-control list
9. Crisis strategy

When you evaluate a crisis and think about how you will approach it strategically, you should ask yourself the following questions:

- What crisis? What actually happened? Are we all interpreting the situation in the same way?
- Is this crisis what it appears to be? Or is there something else behind the crisis? Is this the tip of the iceberg? Can this incident bring the reputation of the whole company, the group and the sector into question? Are our safety standards being questioned? Can other elements of our company be brought into disrepute? How will the company values be interpreted?
- Should we expect still more problems? Will more of this type of environmental problem, explosion, strike, etc, take place?
- What will happen in the worst case? Prepare for the worst-case scenarios.
- How will the public groups and stakeholders interpret this matter? Try to imagine how an outsider would view this crisis. How does the concerned community view this situation? The personnel who have only just learnt what happened? And what about the other public groups, especially the media? What would you think if you were in their position? Can you ask them that question? Have you already thought of calling a couple of journalists to find out whether they think it is an insignificant matter or front-page news?

- Timing? First: when will the media (radio, TV, internet sites, bloggers, daily newspapers, magazines, trade press) begin to report on the incident? Is our information adequate or should we take the time to provide them with more detailed information? And when will we inform the employees, the government and head office? Then: how long will the crisis last? There is the initial incident, and then there are the consequences, the negotiations, the restoration of the situation, contacts with pressure groups, NGOs, etc.

- What is at risk? What will we lose in the worst case? How loyal are our clients, our suppliers and our shareholders? Will they also be loyal in bad times? How long will people remember this incident? What will the impact be on the reputation of our company or organization?

- Can we get the crisis under control? In a general context: how can our actions contribute to speculation and negative or imprecise reporting being limited as quickly as possible and to preventing the crisis from getting out of hand? In a limited context: can the crisis be attributed to a specific branch or product? If you only use the geographical name of the branch or the name of the specific product and you give the spokespeople a role that is limited to the subsidiary, you may be able to keep the name of the parent company and/or its other products out of the line of fire or at least limit the damage.

- Can we find allies? Would our sectoral employers' organization or professional association be better able to communicate the message credibly or ensure that it is received better? Or perhaps an independent research centre or university?

- Who is involved? Are third parties involved with the incident? Are there government services that have not done their jobs properly? Suppliers? An extortionist? Vandals? Terrorists? That can influence our strategy: if we come first with the news, we may be labelled as 'guilty', regardless. It may be possible for you – along with the public – to blame that other 'guilty party' now.

Crisis-control list
10. Crisis communication

What you definitely must communicate in the event of a crisis:

● Details: as much information as possible about the incident or the issue.
● Sympathy: concern, understanding, possibly also regret, possibly apologies.
● Reassurance: 'There is no longer any danger', 'It is not harmful', advice to people who are concerned, 'One chance in a million', etc.
● What are we doing about it? A thorough investigation by an independent body.
● Good reputation of our company: our company has always done so much good.
● Extensive information: where and when will more information be available?
● Possibly: free-phone numbers, help lines, special websites, etc.
● Background information: details about products, procedures, chemicals, the company, etc.

Always give – to the extent that it is possible, of course – details and practical examples. If you only say, 'Our security standards are the best in our sector', that will not be credible. But if you describe how often the ministry of public health or social affairs has investigated your company to the smallest detail, how much your company invests in safety, how many employees are responsible for it, what your company does precisely to ensure safety, that will be credible. This applies to all forms of messages (for example reassurance, good reputation) where your version of the facts will not be accepted at face value.

Appendix 1

Factual information document

COMPANY NAME: ....

Description of company (in no more than eight words)

....

Year founded:

....

Accreditations:

....

Awards: ....

Brand names of products/services in portfolio: ....

....

End-user prices: ....

Your route(s) to market (% of each channel): ....

Trade prices: ....

Typical margins to channel: ....

New products coming through from R&D: ....

....

When? ....

Last year's sales by volume/units: ....

Last year's sales by revenue: ....

This year's sales by volume/units: ....

This year's sales by revenue: ....

Overall size of market:
By volume/units: ....

By revenue $: ....

Your share of market: ....%

Your position in market: ....

Main competitors: ....

....

Your customers:
How many: ....

What sectors: ....

Top customer/user names: ....

Total number of staff:
Worldwide: ....

By region: ....

In sales: ....   In support: ....

In R&D: ....   In admin: ....

Anticipated recruitment this year: ....

Company description:
Describe your company in 100 words or attach existing press release boilerplate here:

....

....

....

....

Contacts:
Main telephone: ....

Free phone: ....

Web address: ....

Main press contact:

Name: ....

E-mail: ....

Office number (plus ext): ....

Mobile: ....

© 2007 NettResults, reproduced with permission.

Appendix 2

Message development document

Message development 1: pre-crisis

	Facts	Message
Company		
Products		
Services		
People		
Customers		

Message development 2: possible crises

Issues	Your Opinion

Message development 3:
how to respond in a crisis

Predictable Questions	Your Response

Appendix 3
Crisis preparation document

Issue	**Company is reported in the press as being fraudulent**
Outcome	Possible loss of reputation
Possible media questions	• Is the fraudulent claim true? • How much money is involved? • Who was involved? • Will the company take legal action against individual employees? • What happened? • Is the company cooperating with any government agencies? • What action is being taken to repair damage? • How can the company ensure this will not be repeated?
Suggested messages	• Honest transparency of any fraudulent claims • Company takes hard line against individual rogue employees • Internal investigation launched immediately and full co-operation with all government agencies • Upon completion of internal investigation all findings will be provided to the press
Pre-approved comments	• We take any fraudulent claim against the company very seriously. At this time our internal legal councillors are looking at the situation with our CEO and we expect to have a further comment for the press by 5pm local time.

There are many situations that can affect a company. For each possible scenario that can be envisioned, a simple form such as the one in the figure should be completed. The more time spent on imagining scenarios in advance, the better prepared your organization will be. Other possible issues could include the following.

Your company

What would happen if:

- The industry you operate in was discredited?
- The area you operate in experiences a natural disaster?

- Your company was accused of committing tax evasion?
- Your company facilities were closed for environmental reasons?

Products

What would happen if:

- One of your products caused a fatality?
- One of your products was identified by the press as suffering from package tampering?
- An unidentified body/animal part was found in one of your products?
- One of your suppliers failed to deliver parts/raw materials needed to meet supply?
- Demand outstripped supply to such a level that there were riots to purchase your products?
- Your products in-store were moving slowly and 'purchase by' dates were being reached before the products were sold?
- Your products were accused of causing damage to unborn children?

Services

What would happen if:

- The media investigated your company over poor service?
- A client/customer brought a legal case against your company for – you name it?
- Your company identified a logistical problem causing wrong shipments?

People

What would happen if:

- Your company's R&D department was exposed for stealing a competitor's trademark?
- Your accounts department was accused of over (or double) charging clients?
- Your CFO was found to be defrauding your company?
- Your founder was found guilty of a domestic crime and sentenced to prison?
- Your director was found guilty of drink driving?

- Your HR director was accused by a staff member of sexual advances?
- A trade union voted for a strike that would cause your workers to down tools?
- A mass walkout of staff causes a loss of production?
- Your company is cited by the press as one of the worst places in town to work?

Customers

What would happen if:

- Your largest client moved to your biggest competitor?
- Your customers refused to pay for services due to poor delivery?
- Your customer lodges a complaint of inappropriate behaviour by one of your sales executives?
- Your customer complains of faulty products and that complaint is picked up by the press?
- Your customer is accused of using your product/service to produce something unlawful?

Unfortunately, the list above is never going to be exhaustive, but the more you work on the most obvious, or most damaging, the better prepared you will be if a crisis does occur.

© 2007 NettResults, reproduced with permission.

Appendix 4

Special considerations for dealing with reporters in a crisis

- Focus on the priorities.
- The first concern *always* is human life – injuries or death.
  - only an incident that involves loss of life should be called a 'tragedy';
  - during the first minutes after an accident, refer only to injuries. Do not report fatalities until an official has pronounced the victims dead;
  - the final consideration is continuation/restoration of operations and services.
- Make the necessary calls as soon as possible, but be aware cell phone conversations may be intercepted.
- Prepare a response statement.
- Avoid descriptive words such as 'catastrophe' or 'fireball'.
- Do not speculate, for example, about the cause of an incident, or appear to assign blame or responsibility.
- Do not estimate damage in monetary terms.
- Never say, 'No comment.' If you can't provide an answer, explain why.
- If you don't know an answer, say, 'At this point, we don't know.'
- Do not release the names of injured or dead until after family members have been notified.
- It's okay to refer to 'the company' and to use 'we'.
- Always assume:
  - the microphone is live;
  - the camera is on; and
  - everything is 'on the record'.

Bibliography

Alaska Airlines website, 13 February 2007

Carson, R (1962) *Silent Spring* (re-issued by Penguin Classics, London, 2000)

Fombrun, C J (1996) *Reputation,* Harvard Business School Press, Harvard, Boston, MA

Fombrun, C J and Van Riel, C B M (2004) *Fame and Fortune,* Prentice Hall, Indianapolis, IN

Hill, D (2003) *Body of Truth,* John Wiley & Sons, Hoboken, NJ

Lawrence, A, Weber, J and Post, J (2005) *Business and Society – Stakeholders, ethics, public policy,* 11th edn, McGraw-Hill Irwin, New York

National Transportation Safety Board website, 13 February 2007

Porter, M E (1985) *Competitive Advantage,* The Free Press, New York

Quinn, F (1990) *Crowning the Customer,* O'Brien Press, Dublin

Ries, A and Ries, L (2004) *The Fall of Advertising and the Rise of PR,* Harper-Collins, New York

Wall Street Journal Online, 17 May 2005

Zadek, S (2004) 'The path to corporate responsibility', *Harvard Business Review*, reference Ro412J, 12 January, 8

Index

NB: page numbers in *italics* indicate figures or tables in the text